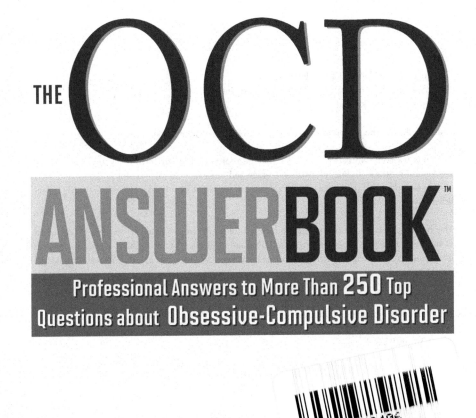

THE OCD
ANSWERBOOK™

Professional Answers to More Than 250 Top Questions about Obsessive-Compulsive Disorder

T0059406

— PATRICK B. McGRATH, PHD —

sourcebooks

Published by Sourcebooks, Inc.
P.O. Box 4410, Naperville, Illinois 60567-4410
(630) 961-3900
Fax: (630) 961-2168
www.sourcebooks.com

Library of Congress Cataloging-in-Publication Data

McGrath, Patrick B.
  The OCD answer book : professional answers to more than 250 top questions about obsessive-compulsive disorder / Patrick B. McGrath.
      p. cm.
  Includes bibliographical references (p.231) and index.
  (trade pbk.)
  1. Obsessive-compulsive disorder--Miscellanea. I. Title. II. Title: OCD answer book.

RC533.M44 2007
616.85'227--dc22

                              2007038239

Printed and bound in the United States of America.
POD 10 9 8 7 6 5

To all of my patients—thank you for allowing me to work with you throughout my career as a student, intern, postdoctoral fellow, and finally, psychologist. Your trust, patience, and courage inspire me to continue to help people with anxiety disorders learn to see fear as just an emotion and not a way of life.

Also, to the memory of Joan Tibbs, my "other mother," and Diane Blackburn, my favorite teacher; I miss you both very much.

Contents

Acknowledgments vii
Introduction ix

Chapter 1. What Is Obsessive-Compulsive Disorder? 1
Chapter 2. Identifying OCD 19
Chapter 3. Causes of OCD 47
Chapter 4. Obsessions 63
Chapter 5. Compulsions 77
Chapter 6. OCD and Its Relationship with Other Disorders . . .91
Chapter 7. Psychological Therapies for OCD 119
Chapter 8. The "OCD Brain" and Medications 163
Chapter 9. Living with OCD 177
Chapter 10. Talking about OCD with Others 203
Chapter 11. Tips for Getting Help 213
Appendix A: Obsession Challenge Worksheet 222
Appendix B: Daily Exposure Homework Sheet 224
Appendix C: Fear Hierarchy 226
Appendix D: The Vertical Arrow 228

Bibliography 231
Index 235
About the Author 241

Acknowledgments

I would like to thank the many people who have influenced my educational and professional development over the past thirty-one years. From some of my earliest teachers, such as Diane Blackburn and Kevin Korschgen, and my most recent mentors, Timothy J. Bruce, Charles L. Spirrison, Peter Gutierrez, Barbara Palombi, and C. Alec Pollard, I have learned many varied and wonderful things, such as how to find a friend in the darkness, what a week of intense practice can do for you, and what psychology can really offer as a career. And to my parents, thank you for instilling a belief in the value of education in me. I appreciate it more than you will ever know.

Thanks also to my many family members, friends, and co-workers who have answered the call and offered me ideas for questions about what they would want to know about OCD, including the following individuals: Adrienne Ahlquist, Shayla Parker, Simon Jencius, Suzanne DeFabiis, Linda Cao, Delores Van Lanen, Kimberly Rothwell, Shawna L. Solsvig, Konstantin Slavin, the staff at Alexian Brothers Behavioral Health Hospital, Kelly Broyles, Linda Segreti, Michael and Darcy Jeneary, Anis McClin, Tammie Jellison, Katie Bowman, Thomas and Kathleen McGrath, Kim Hayes, Corrie Goldberg, Ann Inman, Tony and Vicky Puleo, Chris Vegas, Jeannie Ridings, Bonnie Buratto, Lori Jones, Jeff Ter Molen, Maria De Venuto, Anna Hanuszewicz, Jeremy and Jamie Scranton, Vicki Shaver, Melissa Williams, Lisa Illenberg, Sarah Loeffler, David Norberg, Vic Thorenz, Leslie Harmel, Jeff Lee, Chandra Grabill, David Novicki, Michele Arndt, Clayton Ciha, Priscilla Rose, Amanda Wantroba-Dogan, Dee Byrne, Michael Payne, David Handschke,

Jeremy Caisley, Mark Coronado, Beth Hopfinger, Samantha Cleaver, April Darrow, Sheila Small, Karen Trofimchuk, Jennifer Abel, Mike Hall, Gerald Geringer, Irene Roe, Jonah M., Stephanie K., Paul Ewinger, Courtney Elliott, Robert S. Tibbs Jr., Patrick J. and Mary Ellen McGrath, Margaret Olofson, and Tak, Julia, and Evan Louie.

Various influences and diversions have included Neil Peart, Alex Lifeson, Geddy Lee, *Stargate SG-1* and *Stargate Atlantis*, Saturday Audio, *Lost*, *Heroes*, *Carnivàle*, Paw Paw, *Magic: The Gathering*, Chris-Con, Galena, Wine Expressions, and Sherman's. And, R.I.P. Sunny Brook Farm.

Thanks to Shana Drehs, Erin Nevius, Dojna Shearer, and the rest of the staff at Sourcebooks for their assistance in the development of this project, and thanks to Bubba for the call.

Introduction

Living with obsessive-compulsive disorder (OCD) isn't easy. If you've picked up this book or been given it, you or someone you love is probably struggling with OCD. Although OCD presents itself in all...

You lie down to go to sleep, but before you can nod off, you wonder whether the garage door is shut. Unsure, you ponder that for a few minutes. Finally you decide to just get up and check it. It's closed. Relieved, you think to yourself that you can now get to sleep. But no. As soon as you lie down again, you wonder whether the front door is locked. It probably is, but you're not quite sure. After pondering that thought for a while, you get up again and check the front door, which is locked. Even though you already knew it was locked, you feel a sense of relief because now you don't need to worry about the doors because you have made 100 percent sure that they are locked. Or have you? Maybe you should check one more time just to be really sure—because, can you ever be too sure about the safety of your house or your family? You may even save them from some harm by checking all of the doors one more time. So you go and check again, and again, and again, until you are finally so exhausted that you just fall asleep. But tomorrow night it will start all over again, and it will be just a bit worse and harder to stop than it was tonight.

The preceding scenario is just one example of what it can be like to live with obsessive-compulsive disorder (OCD), an anxiety disorder that affects millions of people in this country. All anxiety disorders are based on an overactivation of the fear system in our brains. With OCD, the fear involves unwanted thoughts, impulses, or images and the attempts to suppress or neutralize them with compulsive behaviors or mental acts. But the obsessions go away for only so long, and when they return, getting rid of them takes a bit more effort than it did the last time. Before you know it, hours of each day are spent engaged in compulsive behaviors, and yet the thoughts, impulses, or images still come.

Luckily there are ways to deal with OCD, and professionals have access to a great deal of information that can help to make the OCD experience easier. *The OCD Answer Book* presents all of this and more, reviewing what OCD is, what types of treatments are available, and how to cope with OCD. I hope that you find this a useful resource and that it can be a stepping-stone for you to further investigate productive living with OCD. Whether you have been diagnosed with OCD, wonder whether you may have OCD, or know someone who has OCD, this book will address some of the questions you may have, and I hope it will help remove some of the mystery surrounding the disorder.

Finally, while you're reading, keep this phrase in the back of your mind: *Anxiety is not a fear of a thing; it is a fear of the way we think about a thing.*

Chapter 1

WHAT IS OBSESSIVE-COMPULSIVE DISORDER?

- What is obsessive-compulsive disorder (OCD)?
- What is an obsession?
- What is a compulsion?
- How many people suffer from OCD?
- Isn't OCD just a lack of willpower or an impulsivity problem?
- Are there different types of OCD?
- How serious is OCD?
- What are the ranges of severity of OCD?
- How does OCD work in the brain?
- Does the media at all influence the prevalence of OCD?
- Is it possible to "grow out" of OCD?
- Does OCD run in families?
- Who has more problems with OCD, men or women?
- Are people with OCD crazy or abnormal?
- Isn't this just the "new" ADHD? Everyone had that a few years ago, and now it seems like everyone has OCD—why is that?
- Is OCD a new disorder, or has it been around for a long time?
- Has the incidence of OCD increased in the past decade?
- How accurately are people with OCD portrayed in the media?
- Are there famous people who have or had OCD?

What is obsessive-compulsive disorder (OCD)?

Obsessive-compulsive disorder (OCD) is an anxiety disorder, according to the *DSM-IV-TR* (the *Diagnostic and Statistical Manual of Mental Disorders, Fourth Edition, Text Revision* (2000)), which is the book that lists and classifies all mental disorders. Anxiety disorders make their sufferers feel disproportionately anxious or fearful, and the main anxiety triggers for people with OCD are obsessive thoughts, images, or impulses that are intrusive and inappropriate and that cause a great deal of distress. They are obsessive because they are unwanted, and a person experiences them over and over again. As a response to these obsessions, a person performs compulsive behaviors in an attempt to somehow get rid of or neutralize the obsessions. Further, these compulsive behaviors go well beyond what would be necessary in everyday life to actually deal with the themes of the obsessive thoughts, impulses, or images. Unfortunately, the compulsions relieve the anxiety only temporarily, and the obsessions return, causing the cycle to play over and over again throughout the day. Let's look at an example:

> Obsession: "I just touched a doorknob. What if the person who touched it before me had HIV? Now I might have it as well."
> Leading to . . .
> Compulsion: Hand washing, possibly for 15 minutes with very hot water and vigorous scrubbing.
> Ten minutes later . . .
> Obsession: "I just flushed a toilet. What if the person who flushed the toilet before me had HIV? Now I might have it as well."
> Leading to . . .
> Compulsion: Hand washing, possibly for 15 minutes with very hot water and vigorous scrubbing.

These obsessions can occur ten to twenty-five times a day, or even more frequently, and the compulsive behaviors that follow help the person relieve the anxiety brought on by the thought. The behavior is very excessive, however, and seems to work only for a short period of time. Then the obsessions typically return, and the cycle starts all over again.

What is an obsession?

An obsession is a thought, impulse, or image that appears in someone's mind and causes that person severe anxiety or distress. Obsessions are the hidden part of OCD because no one but the OCD sufferer can experience the obsessions or the turmoil that the obsessions generate. Not only can others not witness the obsessions, but additionally, the individuals experiencing them often do not want to share their obsessions because of their disturbing nature.

Let's take an example: Imagine walking down the street, stepping on a crack, and remembering the old saying "step on a crack and break your mother's back." Most people would just ignore this or recognize it as a meaningless saying. A person with OCD, however, may start to think about the saying and wonder why someone would say such a thing. *Could it be because it is true? Could stepping on a crack really break my mother's back?*

This thought might play over and over ceaselessly in the person's head, and as it does, the person will start believing more and more that it could be true and thinking how horrible it would be. People with OCD give their random thoughts a lot of credence, and they start to imagine greater and greater probabilities that the things they fear might actually happen, despite the true probability of their happening. They can recognize that their thoughts are illogical, but they feel overwhelmed by them. As their fear of a thought increases, they increasingly attempt to somehow get rid of the thought.

One way people with OCD attempt to get rid of a thought is to suppress it—they tell themselves not to think of it, or they just try to ignore it. Unfortunately, this is often as unsuccessful as trying to get a song out of your head that you have been singing all day by trying not to think about it. Therefore, they may also try to actually do something to get rid of the obsession—enter the compulsion. (We go into more detail on obsessions in Chapter 4.)

What is a compulsion?

A compulsion (also called a ritual) is a person's attempt to get rid of an obsessive thought, impulse, or image. Continuing with the sidewalk example in the previous question, the person may try to go back to the sidewalk and walk over the crack, as a way to undo the previous act of stepping on the crack. Or the person may recite a prayer or a special saying over and over again, such as "I love my mother," as a way to counteract the fact that, the person believes, he may have just broken his mother's back. Often, once the compulsion is performed in what the person deems the right way, there is a sense of relief, and the person moves on and continues his or her day. As the OCD progresses, however, the periods of relief get shorter and shorter, and people who suffer from OCD engage in rituals more and more often.

A compulsion could also be a behavior or mental act that a person feels compelled to perform in a very strict fashion, even without the experience of an obsession. Some people may do things each day in a certain way because they believe that that is just the right way to do it, even though they may not be able to explain why—it just feels right. An example of this may be someone who straightens pictures on walls, even if that person is not at his or her own home. A picture being askew is disturbing to the person, and they may feel compelled to straighten the picture even at the risk of offending the person whose possessions he or she is touching. To the person suffering from OCD, that risk is worth taking to stop the discomfort of seeing a picture that is not hanging straight.

Compulsions are outward signs of OCD—outsiders can see OCD sufferers washing their hands, turning lights on and off, checking door locks, and so on. Yet OCD is not always external; mental compulsions can also occur, such as having to say a prayer the correct way a certain number of times to prevent punishment from a higher power. (We go into more detail on compulsions in Chapter 5.)

How many people suffer from OCD?

According to the National Institute of Mental Health, 2.2 million Americans are diagnosed with OCD. The Obsessive Compulsive Foundation website (www.ocfoundation.org) states that 1 in 40 adults and 1 in 200 children have OCD, which adds up to about 5 million people with OCD in the United States. And the *DSM-IV-TR* (2000) states that the lifetime prevalence (the number of people in the United States who have a disorder sometime over the course of their life) of OCD is 2.5 percent. Given a population of almost 300 million Americans, approximately 7.5 million people in the United States alone will experience OCD over the course of their lifetime.

Isn't OCD just a lack of willpower or an impulsivity problem?

Actually, it is neither of these. If it were a lack of willpower, then a good lecture or a verbal thrashing ought to be plenty to get someone to just give it up and gain the needed "moral fortitude" to be fine. If it were an impulsivity problem, then we would see impulsivity in numerous areas, not just in the compulsions that characterize a particular case of OCD.

OCD is a mental disorder that affects the deepest parts of a person's brain. It is not something that can just be wished away or punished into submission. It is, however, a disorder that can be treated, and people with OCD can learn to live healthy and productive lives.

Are there different types of OCD?

There really are not different types of OCD, but there are different areas where OCD thoughts and behaviors may be concentrated. Some of these areas include the following:

- **Washing and cleaning:** If you compulsively wash and clean, you may have a fear of either getting contaminated or passing a contaminant on to others. To counteract this, you might engage in excessive washing and cleaning to try to remove any germs that were received or could be passed on (e.g., washing your hands with alcohol every time you take the garbage out).

- **Hoarding:** You may resist throwing out items because such objects could have a possible use in the future. A variation of this includes having difficulty getting rid of items because money was spent on them, or maybe some meaning is associated with the objects, and thus losing them would mean the loss of a memory (e.g., losing a souvenir T-shirt from my 1988 stay at Sunny Brook Farm will mean that I will forget all about my vacation).

- **Checking:** This compulsion includes needing to repeatedly check items such as locks, windows, doors, or potentially dangerous appliances (e.g., stoves) to be sure they are safe, locked, or secured in order to prevent damage to yourself or others (for instance, checking 10 times to make sure the windows are locked so that no one can break into your home).

- **Scrupulosity:** The fears associated with scrupulosity deal with the possibility that you have somehow offended a higher power. The resulting compulsive behaviors that you perform (constant praying, confessing, and so on) are designed to get you back into the good graces of that higher power.

- **Aggression:** The fear of harming others often results in compulsive behaviors to ensure that you do not, or did not, actually hurt anyone (e.g., not allowing your own children to sit on your lap for fear that you may molest them).

How serious is OCD?

OCD is a very serious disorder. In fact, of all the mental health disorders, it is considered one of the most serious in terms of the amount of burden it causes the population of the world, according to the World Health Organization. This is a result of several factors, including the number of people who are affected by it (2.3–2.5 percent of the population of the world), the ability of OCD to affect people across the age spectrum (from children through senior citizens), the difficulty in finding specialized treatment, and the often devastating effects it can have on people who suffer from it.

What are the ranges of severity of OCD?

Some people with OCD may have only a few symptoms and may never seek treatment (many family members or friends would just say that they have a few odd or quirky behaviors, such as always turning off the gas and water lines in the house when they leave to go to work, just to be sure that there are no fires or floods). Others may suffer from OCD so severely that they engage in behaviors that are highly painful or isolating. For example, some individuals shower for over twenty-four hours straight to wash off germs, live in only one room of their home for years to avoid spreading any contamination, or go to confession on a daily basis because they are afraid that they might have committed a sin. At its most severe level, OCD may require residential treatment, which can take from thirty to ninety days or more. Although this is the extreme end of the spectrum, individuals with OCD even this severe can benefit from treatment from OCD specialists.

How does OCD work in the brain?

We are just beginning to know how OCD works in the brain, and it will probably take decades before we really have a clear idea. That said, this is one of the most hotly contested questions in psychology and psychiatry today.

Two camps of scientists are currently researching how OCD actually works in the brain. Researchers who focus on medicine and brain imaging (PET scans, magnetic imaging, etc.) are attempting to find exactly how brain structures "talk" using neurotransmitters (chemical messengers) to discover what the communication differences are between the brains of people who do and do not have OCD. It is their hope that by discovering what areas of the brain are active and what chemicals are being released when someone is experiencing an obsession or compulsion, they will be able to develop medical procedures or medications that will combat OCD.

The other camp of research is interested in developing talk and behavioral therapies for OCD. Their basic focus is on how a thought becomes an obsession and why people develop the compulsions that they perform in response to the obsession. Because it will probably take a long time for the first camp to develop the technologies that may be required for specific medications or surgeries, this second group is interested in developing therapies that can be implemented in the near future; therapies based on the types of thoughts that individuals with OCD have and the behaviors they perform.

The goal of both camps is to develop the best forms of treatment, and it is hoped that someday a combination of medical and behavioral therapies will be designed to best treat OCD.

Does the media at all influence the prevalence of OCD?

It does to some extent, but not always in a bad way. Now that drug companies are advertising medications, people are more aware of certain symptoms and are going to their doctors and asking questions. It is great that we have such a well-informed consumer public.

However, we may be overinformed. For example, while we were growing up, most of our mothers did not bleach all of our toys, the whole family drank out of the same glass bottle of soda pop, we used a bar of regular soap at the sink, and we held shopping cart handles with no fear. Now we are told on television commercials to bleach everything to kill all of the bad germs; rarely do you see people sharing a drink anymore; soaps are liquid, and almost all of them are antibacterial; and we have wipes (supposedly as an advertisement) at the grocery store for our cart handles.

If these things were really as dangerous as we've recently decided that they are, how did anyone older than twenty survive to be older than twenty? No one has ever heard of a mass illness linked to shopping cart handles, yet we are becoming paranoid about merely touching things others have touched.

The downside of all this is our children will probably get sicker over time because their immune systems will not have been given the chance to fight certain bacteria and viruses. Also, we are going to create more and more drug-resistant germs, which will be what really end up causing us harm—the very things we are doing to protect ourselves may be the things that hurt us in the end!

So really, media is a double-edged sword when it comes to OCD. Although it does encourage people to get the help they need, it also fosters an aura of paranoia that is unfounded and can lead to a lot of worrying and potential OCD symptoms.

Is it possible to "grow out" of OCD?

There is not any research supporting the idea that you can grow out of OCD. Despite this, many patients resist seeking therapy because they hope their OCD will just pass. When this doesn't happen (and in many cases, OCD worsens over time), they finally enter therapy.

Once people with OCD are in therapy, however, there is a significant chance for them to see improvements in their symptoms. They can learn how to handle the obsessions and resist doing the rituals, allowing for a life that is not controlled by their OCD. Though people will not grow out of their OCD or be able to ignore it into submission, therapy, medications, or a combination of both can help them learn coping strategies and behavioral changes that can, at least outwardly, seem like a cure.

Does OCD run in families?

This question is currently under investigation. Studies conducted by Johns Hopkins Medical Institute have found some possible genetic markers for OCD on several different chromosomes (1, 6, 7, 15, and two markers on chromosome 3). There were more abnormalities in these chromosomes for people who had OCD than there were for people who did not have OCD.

Other studies corroborate the theory that OCD has a genetic component. Identical twins with OCD show about a 65–85 percent concordance rate (if one twin has OCD, the other also does), whereas fraternal twins show only about a 35–45 percent concordance rate. This suggests that the "identical genes" of the identical twins share something that could lead to the development of OCD more so than do the "non-identical genes" of the fraternal twins. Therefore, identical twins with OCD must share something in their genetic code that leads them both to develop OCD more readily than fraternal twins. However, this also shows that it is not purely genetic, because if it was, then the identical twins would have to have a 100 percent concordance rate. Therefore, there must also be some environmental influences that lead to the development of OCD.

To date, no single OCD gene has been found, and there probably is not one specific gene that is responsible for OCD. More likely, a combination of genetic markers and environmental occurrences are required for the development of OCD.

Who has more problems with OCD, men or women?

According to the *DSM-IV-TR* (2000), the only gender difference is that males, on average, develop OCD earlier than females. Otherwise, the course and the prevalence of OCD appear the same across genders.

Are people with OCD crazy or abnormal?

No.

People who have OCD do have a mental disorder, and unfortunately some people still think that having a mental disorder means a person is "nuts." These people probably also think that you could just gain control of your OCD and stop it if you would just put your mind to it. If it were that easy, there would be no mental disorders in the world! Instead, mental disorders are very real and very debil-itating. People with mental disorders are often silent sufferers because many of them hide their difficulties and either do not get treatment or put off getting treatment until the effects of their dis-order are very severe. Actions that might be socially interpreted as "crazy" could be the symptoms of an untreated disorder.

As for "abnormal," that word typically has negative connotations, and yet there are many things that are abnormal that we consider good. For example, being a genius is abnormal, given that only a very small percentage of the population meets the criteria for genius-level intelligence. But we consider this abnormality a good thing. So, although having OCD is abnormal, abnormality is not an inherently bad thing.

This question really boils down to what many people think but few ask—are people with OCD (and other mental disorders) bad people? The answer is no; they are people suffering from a problem that is treatable, and they have the ability to live happy and produc-tive lives.

Isn't this just the "new" ADHD? Everyone had that a few years ago, and now it seems like everyone has OCD—why is that?

The seeming recent surge in OCD may be a result of several factors. First, there is less stigma attached to mental health problems now than even five years ago. The more people learn about mental health difficulties, the more people understand that sufferers have as much control over OCD as they do brain tumors or gestational diabetes. Some things can be done to prevent the onset of these difficulties, but we can never guarantee 100 percent prevention. And because more people are now talking about mental health concerns, it may seem that some disorders are more prevalent than they were five or ten years ago, but this is just an effect of more people openly entering treatment for mental health issues.

Second, several movies featuring OCD have been released in the last few years, and there was even a 2005 special on MTV called *True Life: I Have OCD*. OCD is a very intriguing disorder to many people, and its popularity may come from its peculiarity. People are fascinated by hearing stories about hour-long hand washings or a deep need to arrange all of the labels in the cupboards a certain way every day. Also, hearing about OCD doesn't often trigger the same kinds of sad feelings that hearing about depression does, and OCD stories often don't contain the kind of violence that can accompany psychotic disorders. Thus, it seems safe and almost entertaining to discuss.

Third, there has been a push by national organizations to get people with OCD the help that they need. The Obsessive Compulsive Foundation has started a major media campaign for children and teens to spread the word about OCD and to let them know what treatments are available. On its website (www.ocfoundation.org), viewers can see an 18-year-old female named Elizabeth talk on a streaming video about being the face of OCD. She looks like any other person, yet she has OCD. The goal of the campaign is to let people know that OCD can affect anyone and that help is available to everyone. The Obsessive Compulsive Foundation of Chicago also has some great information on its website (www.OCDChicago.org).

Finally, the consumer public is becoming more informed. There has been an explosion of information concerning mental disorders in the last few years via the Internet and on daily talk shows. Although you should always be on the lookout for the great deal of misinformation and misrepresentations out there, the fact that people can research their own problems is helping to spread the word about what OCD is and what can be done to help sufferers.

Is OCD a new disorder, or has it been around for a long time?

OCD is not a new disorder. In fact, OCD has been written about for centuries—as far back as the sixth century. According to Ian Osborn in his book *Tormenting Thoughts and Secret Rituals* (1999), there are numerous references to what we now call OCD in early religious and Greek writings. Many of the early mentions of OCD are about scrupulosity, which makes sense, given that most of the individuals who could read and write at that time were philosophers, monks, and priests.

Ministers such as Richard Baxter in the 1600s and John Baptist Scaramelli in 1753 wrote excellent advice on obsessive thoughts, both telling readers not to fight the thoughts because that only makes the thoughts stronger, but to instead just accept the thoughts and move on with their day.

Not until Pierre Janet, a French psychiatrist in the nineteenth and twentieth centuries, was OCD actually written about by its name as we know it today, in his work *Obsessions and Psychasthenia*. Similar to the earlier religious writers, he suggested that individuals expose themselves to their fears.

Sadly, just as this work was published in 1903, Freud's writings on psychoanalysis were becoming popular, and therapy for OCD was set back 50 years. Instead of encouraging individuals to confront their fears head on, Freud's style of therapy encouraged people to confront their unconscious thoughts and impulses only in their heads. People spent years lying on couches talking about everything that came into their minds so that an analyst could interpret all of their thoughts and dreams and try to come up with why they were experiencing the difficulties they had in their lives. This did absolutely nothing to help OCD; for people suffering from a cognitive and behavioral problem, only discussing their fears did not help get their obsessions or compulsions in check.

Finally, in the 1960s, psychoanalysis came under research scrutiny and was found to have no support, and behavior therapy (see Chapter 7) made huge strides in treatment effectiveness. Ever since then, it has been the main form of therapy for OCD and the most research-supported treatment for it as well.

Has the incidence of OCD increased in the past decade?

Most likely the incidence of OCD has not increased in the last decade—what has increased is an awareness of it. As more therapists become familiar with OCD and how to treat it, there will be more diagnoses of OCD. But just because more people are diagnosed with OCD does not mean that the incidence of it is increasing—people diagnosed with OCD would have had it regardless of whether it was recognized by a doctor or not. Though more people may be diagnosed correctly with OCD, there will most likely be a decrease in the diagnoses that OCD might have been otherwise diagnosed as, such as tic disorders (see Chapter 6). This will be an interesting area for future research.

This is currently happening with autism and mental retardation. While many families who have children diagnosed with autism are saying that the diagnosis of autism is on an alarmingly increasing upswing, the diagnosis of mental retardation appears to be on a steep decline (Croen, Grether, Hoogstrate, and Selvin, 2004). This may be because those children who were once diagnosed with mental retardation are now being more accurately diagnosed with autism. As we continue to learn more about individual disorders and how to differentiate them, statistics will shift in many areas.

How accurately are people with OCD portrayed in the media?

Several recent movies and TV shows have showcased OCD. Currently, *Monk*, a show airing on cable, portrays a detective with OCD. The writers of *Monk* consult with the Anxiety Disorders Association of America for information on how to accurately depict the disorder.

Several recent movies have also featured main characters with OCD, including *The Aviator*, which told the story of the life of Howard Hughes. In 1997, Jack Nicholson portrayed a man with OCD in *As Good as It Gets*. More recently, an independent film called *Dirty Filthy Love* featured a man with OCD and Tourette's syndrome. One of the writers of this film has OCD, so the movie was an especially revealing look at the disorder.

As with any mass media portrayal of a disorder, some symptoms are exaggerated for effect, and others are minimized. For example, many people think of hand washing when they think of OCD, and thus this image is perpetuated in the media. But these portrayals often fail to capture the inner turmoil that many people with OCD suffer as they attempt to fight their obsessions and challenge their compulsions. They know that what they are doing is illogical; they just feel helpless to do anything about it—but this is rarely discussed.

Are there famous people who have or had OCD?

Howard Hughes may be one of the most famous people to have had OCD. The multimillionaire movie producer and aviation expert was said to sort his peas by size before he would eat them, and he had an air filtration system built into the trunk of his car so that he would not have to breathe unclean air. Biographers have also said that he was consumed with the minor details of things, often delaying projects and movies until they were "just right." Toward the end of his life, he isolated himself from people because of his fears of contamination.

Mark Summers, who once hosted *Double Dare* on Nickelodeon, has written a book about his struggles with OCD. He described in an interview how he would get on the floor with a comb to make all of the fibers on the carpet go a certain way.

Howie Mandel, host of *Deal or No Deal*, has talked about his OCD in several interviews. One of his fears is illness: If a family member gets ill, he moves into the other of two homes he has on his property. Also notice that he never shakes hands on *Deal or No Deal*—he only touches fists. He does this so that he does not have to deal with any obsessions about his hands being dirty while taping the show.

Chapter 2

IDENTIFYING OCD

- How do you diagnose an obsession?
- How do you diagnose a compulsion?
- Are there any other criteria for the diagnosis of OCD besides obsessions and compulsions?
- At what age does OCD develop? How early can it be diagnosed?
- What are the early manifestations of OCD?
- What is the difference between a habit and an OCD ritual?
- What exams or tests are used to diagnose OCD?
- How accurate are those tests?
- Can OCD be diagnosed with a physical exam?
- How many obsessions and compulsions are typical for a person with OCD?
- Does your medical history play a part in OCD?
- What are some common fears and beliefs that people with OCD have?
- Are people with OCD fixated on cleanliness and, if so, why?
- Does the course of OCD stay the same, steadily get worse, improve, or vary over time?
- Where is the line drawn between having a set pattern of doing things (such as household chores) and OCD?
- Can a ritual be compulsively *not* doing something?
- I am a perfectionist—is that OCD?
- Is there such a thing as situational OCD—is it possible to be obsessive about only one thing?
- Do people with OCD fear bodily fluids?
- I really like the Sci-Fi Channel—people say I am obsessed with it. Does this mean I have OCD?
- I am in high school and have a huge crush on this football player. I can't stop thinking of him—I even dream of him! Do I have OCD?
- Do athletes have OCD when they perform good-luck rituals before each game, like drinking the same kind of soda or putting on the same dirty socks?
- Many children develop certain routines or want things done in very specific ways—is this OCD or just a normal part of growing up?

- What's the difference between someone with OCD and someone who just likes to be organized?
- What are the most common symptoms of OCD?
- How do you tell the difference between true OCD and simple obsessive thinking?
- What are some typical themes of obsessions?
- What if someone likes the thoughts he keeps having over and over—is that OCD?
- What are some examples of checking obsessions and compulsions?
- What are some examples of contamination obsessions and compulsions?
- What are some examples of hoarding obsessions and compulsions?
- What are some examples of symmetry obsessions and compulsions?
- What are some examples of scrupulosity obsessions and compulsions?
- What are some examples of harm obsessions?
- Do people with OCD really have control over their disorder but just do it to get attention?

How do you diagnose an obsession?

An obsession diagnosis requires that four criteria be met. First, the obsession is defined as a persistent and repetitive thought, impulse, or image that, according to the *DSM-IV-TR* (2000), is intrusive and inappropriate and causes significant anxiety and distress. Next, the obsession must not be just worries about real life problems. Things that most people would reasonably worry about do not count as an obsession—the concern must go beyond what we would normally expect, such as washing your very dirty laundry one time on an extended cycle versus washing all of your laundry four times before you wear it again, just to be sure that it is clean. Third, the person either must try to ignore or suppress the obsession or must try to neutralize it with another thought or action (a compulsive behavior). Finally, the person must recognize that the obsession is a product of his or her own mind—it is not a psychotic experience such as a hallucination of hearing voices telling you to fear something. A person must be able to say that he or she recognizes that he or she is having obsessive thoughts, but is having trouble dealing with them.

How do you diagnose a compulsion?

A compulsion, according to the *DSM-IV-TR* (2000), must meet two criteria: First, the compulsion must be a behavioral or mental act that a person feels that he or she must perform in response to an obsession or according to certain rigid rules. Second, these behaviors or mental acts are performed either to reduce distress or to prevent a dreaded consequence from happening. Further, these acts are clearly excessive or are not connected in a realistic or logical way with what the person is attempting to neutralize or prevent (e.g., counting to one hundred to prevent a bomb from going off somewhere in the world).

Are there any other criteria for the diagnosis of OCD besides obsessions and compulsions?

When mental health professionals attempt to make the diagnosis of OCD, they're going to want to make sure that the obsessions or compulsions are not better accounted for by another disorder. For example, individuals with eating disorders have many rituals about how they will eat or touch food, but that may be more a result of the eating disorder than of OCD. (It's true that a person could have both diagnoses as well, which is why a professional needs to conduct a thorough interview with the patient and the patient's significant other, family, or friends.)

Also, the amount of time spent ritualizing is important. If the rituals do not take up much time in a person's day (under an hour), a diagnosis of OCD may not be appropriate. Or if the obsessive thoughts are not significant enough to cause much distress, or if the person is unable to recognize that the compulsions are excessive (this does not apply to children), then an OCD diagnosis may not be warranted. At least one of the above criteria (time, significant distress, or recognition) has to be present for a diagnosis of OCD.

Basically, the effects of the obsessions and compulsions need to be significant enough to cause a lot of distress in a person's life, to be not better accounted for by another mental health disorder, and to be recognized by the person as excessive, even though the person feels compelled to perform them anyway. If people do meet some, but not all, of the criteria for OCD, then the diagnosis of anxiety disorder not otherwise specified (NOS) would be appropriate. A person could still get treated for the OCD-like symptoms, even if he or she did not meet the full criteria for OCD.

At what age does OCD develop? How early can it be diagnosed?

OCD can be diagnosed in childhood, as early as ages five or six. Males typically develop OCD earlier than females—boys tend to develop OCD between the ages of 6 and 15, whereas females typically develop OCD in their late teens and early twenties. The majority of people who develop OCD show signs of it before the age of 25, and very few new cases of OCD occur after the age of 50. Recent research has shown that new parents are also at a higher than average risk of OCD, possibly because of the increased stress that having a baby can bring to their lives and their possible obsessive focus on the safety of their new child.

What are the early manifestations of OCD?

The first signs of OCD might occur internally (obsessions) or externally (compulsions). A person with OCD may start to notice that he is having difficulties getting rid of certain thoughts, or the people around him (often parents) may start to notice that he is performing certain rituals. What these early manifestations of OCD actually are depends on the type of OCD that a person may have. If it is scrupulosity, the OCD may manifest in mostly obsessions, such as thoughts of offending a higher power and the resulting compulsive prayer, whereas someone who fears that others may be in danger may do many behavioral compulsions, such as checking outlets and pilot lights.

The early manifestations of OCD are as broad and varied as full-blown OCD, but one commonality is that usually only a few symptoms are noticeable in people as the OCD first develops, and then the symptoms become more and more visible as the disorder continues.

What is the difference between a habit and an OCD ritual?

A habit is something that you do without even thinking about it. It is done without any anxiety, and it is not related to any obsessions. A ritual, in contrast, is performed in order to neutralize an obsession. Often, the person performing the ritual would like to not do the ritual, but he or she feels compelled to do it in order to feel relief from the obsessive thought, impulse, or image. You may know someone who spends a great deal of time making sure that his or her tires are "perfectly" straight when parking the car or someone who arranges his or her desktop items at 90 degree angles. They may do this because they would not be able to stop thinking about the items being out of place or the tires being crooked, or it may give them such an uncomfortable feeling that they feel they have to straighten them. Either way, the straightening is done to relieve some type of uncomfortable feeling generated by the obsessive thought. Others with neatness habits may also like to straighten things, but if they were unable to, it would not affect their day, or they would not feel compelled to go back and fix it, as a person with OCD would.

What exams or tests are used to diagnose OCD?

Many tests have been developed to assess OCD. The most cited test is the Yale-Brown Obsessive Compulsive Scale (Y-BOCS). The Y-BOCS consists of 10 questions that are administered by a clinician in an interview format. The answers are rated on a five-point scale, and scores can range from 0 to 40, with a possible 20 points coming from both the obsession section and the other 20 possible points coming from the compulsion section. The higher the score, the more severe the OCD. Typically, a score of 16 or higher is considered the cutoff for research studies on OCD, so that would be considered a moderate level of OCD. The Y-BOCS also has a 102-item checklist that when administered can review many different subsets of OCD, including the following examples of obsessions and compulsions: contamination, safety, religion, symmetry, hoarding, cleaning, checking, arranging, counting, and confessing.

Other tests may include the Padua Inventory, the Maudsley Obsessional Compulsive Inventory, and the Obsessive Compulsive Inventory. For a full review of the above tests and others for the assessment of OCD, you can consult the *Practitioner's Guide to Empirically Based Measures of Anxiety* (Antony, Orsillo, and Roemer, 2001).

How accurate are those tests?

A test's accuracy can be measured according to several factors. First, do the items measure what they are intended to measure? You would probably not include a question about a person's favorite radio program in a test for OCD. Second, how do the items (questions, activities, and requirements) in a test relate to each other? If they do not relate to each other, it will be difficult to tell how they might group together, which is necessary in order to establish a trend in answers that will help the practitioner come up with a diagnosis. Returning to the previous example, a question about a person's favorite radio program would not be related to a question about a person's hand-washing habits. However, looking at hand-washing habits and sink-cleaning habits could help determine whether there is an obsession there. Third, does the test help distinguish between individuals who have an established diagnosis of OCD and those who do not? If there are no differences in scores between people who have OCD and people free from a mental disorder or people with a mental disorder that is not OCD, then the test is useless.

This is, of course, a very basic overview of checking for test accuracy, but it can give you an idea of what mental health professionals are looking for. All of the tests listed in the answer to the question preceding this one are considered reliable and valid measures of OCD because they have been developed by experts in the field, and evaluation in clinical trials has proven them accurate predictors of who does or does not have OCD or how severe a person's OCD is.

Can OCD be diagnosed with a physical exam?

No, there is not a physical exam that can be used to diagnose OCD. It is possible, however, that some physical symptoms may alert doctors to the possibility that you have OCD, such as blistered or cracked skin from excessive washing; injuries from repetitive motions, such as making the sign of the cross every time you have a "bad" thought; or exhaustion from lack of sleep because of all the time required to perform your compulsive behaviors.

How many obsessions and compulsions are typical for a person with OCD?

That varies with each person with OCD. You may have only one or two obsessions or compulsions, whereas others may spend their entire day anxious and using behaviors to combat their thoughts. What researchers do know from the OCD field trials for the DSM-IV (Foa & Kozak, 1995) is that about 96 percent of patients appear to have both obsessions and compulsions, with only 2 percent reporting only obsessions and 2 percent reporting only compulsions. Further, 30 percent of patients have predominantly obsessions (with some compulsions), 21 percent have predominantly compulsions (with some obsessions), and 49 percent had a relatively equal mix of obsessions and compulsions. Further, research has shown us what the most popular themes are for obsessions (contamination, harming oneself or others, and symmetry are the top three) and compulsions (checking, cleaning/washing, and repeating things are the top three).

Does your medical history play a part in OCD?

Medical history can play a role in the development of OCD. Some research has linked the development of some cases of OCD to a strep throat infection (PANDAS; see question on page 38), whereas other research suggests that there may be a genetic link. Also, alternative treatment research suggests that diet and exercise may play a role because they have been found to have a positive impact on mood disorders such as depression (see Chapter 6).

What are some common fears and beliefs that people with OCD have?

People with OCD believe that the obsessive thoughts, impulses, or images that they experience are much more than mere thoughts, impulses, or images—they think these things are not merely random occurrences, but horrible warnings of some awful event. That is why people with OCD feel such a need to perform compulsive behaviors; they believe they're preventing something catastrophic from happening. (Remember the "step on a crack, break your mother's back" example from the first chapter.)

The other common belief with OCD is that a compulsive behavior has to be performed. People with OCD convince themselves that these behaviors have to be performed either to neutralize an obsession or to have things done the "right" way. Of course, even if they did not do things perfectly, they would be fine, but they have difficulty accepting that or dealing with the thoughts that their inaction would spark about leaving something imperfect.

Are people with OCD fixated on cleanliness and, if so, why?

People with OCD may be obsessed with cleanliness, but this is just one area in which OCD can be focused. According to Foa and Kozak (1995), in their study tracking OCD prevalence, cleaning compulsions are present for about 27 percent of individuals with OCD, and fear of contamination, which is often related to cleaning, is present in about 38 percent of individuals with OCD. Cleanliness may represent several things to people with OCD. Obviously, it may be a physical cue that there are no germs in the vicinity, which may be relieving to them. Without any visible soiling or mess, they may feel that there is nothing in the room that can harm them. Cleanliness may also represent order, and order is often related to control. As long as their possessions are in order, they may feel in control of their environment. Finally, cleanliness may represent avoidance (see Chapter 3 for more information on avoidance behaviors). Some people may clean a room and then never step foot in it again. It may have taken them so long to get the room "just right" that they do not want to risk having to go through all of that cleaning and straightening again, so it becomes something like a museum—only to be admired and never to be used.

Does the course of OCD stay the same, steadily get worse, improve, or vary over time?

There is no standard course that OCD typically runs, but the disorder most often stays roughly the same (some periods of feeling better and some of feeling worse) or gradually gets worse over time. As with any mental disorder or physical ailment, there can be spontaneous recovery, but this is a very rare occurrence. It's also very rare for OCD to come and go—you probably wouldn't meet the criteria for OCD for a few months, then no longer meet the criteria, and then slide back into meeting the criteria again. What's most common is always meeting the criteria for OCD, but at varying levels of intensity, depending on how stressful life is at the time.

Where is the line drawn between having a set pattern of doing things (such as household chores) and having OCD?

We all have set patterns and routines that we follow in our lives— they make things easier for us. If we had to come up with a new way to drive to work, brush our teeth, or read the newspaper each day, our lives would be very stressful—because we would approach everyday tasks as if we had never done them before. So, our patterns help us to do things efficiently.

Therefore, performing a chore in a certain way each time you do it does not mean that you have OCD. However, if you think that the way you do the chore is the only way to do it, only you can do it correctly, and it must be done at set intervals, then it's possible that

OCD is playing a role in the completion of the chore. The easiest way to differentiate OCD and a set pattern would be to imagine not being able to do the chore the set way. If that would not bother you, then OCD is not playing a role. If it would bother you, then OCD may be involved. If this is the case, then you have some choices— you could just live with it, or you could seek some treatment to help you to break the cycle of obsessions and compulsions.

Can a ritual be compulsively *not* doing something?

Yes, this can be an OCD symptom. Although many people think that a ritual involves doing something, it can also involve compulsively and repeatedly not doing something due to a fear of that thing. For example, refusing to sit on a chair without a towel between it and you is probably a compulsion borne of a fear of contamination, and the towel represents either a way to not get contaminated or a way to prevent the spread of contamination to other surfaces. People with OCD may fear that without the towel, contaminants will get on them and somehow harm them, or that they will spread contaminants to others, unknowingly harming them.

Let's separate these two issues to discuss them more in-depth. People who are afraid of contamination are, at the most basic level, worried that they will be harmed. This can come in the form of an illness or disease, or also in the form of a bad feeling. Think of this almost like "cooties"—when children touch something or someone they do not like or think is gross, they say that person or thing has cooties. Performing an action that they fear can give a person with OCD that feeling of having "cooties," but multiplied hundreds of times.

People with OCD may also perceive that the essence of someone is on an item, and if they were to touch that item, or sit on a chair that the person sat on, that person's essence would be on them, and they find that very uncomfortable. They do not necessarily dislike the person—it could be that they just do not know the person or where the person has been, so they think the worst about the person, such as that he or she is contaminated. They would rather sit on a towel to prevent their clothes or body from coming into direct contact with something that they find disgusting—they are unable to see the chair as just a chair that in no way can transmit anything to them. This may sound strange to people without OCD, but people with OCD often irrationally attribute good or bad feelings to different people or things and then do not want to have anything to do with the "bad people." Their rituals are designed to protect them from any physical or mental harm or contamination, whether the ritual is doing something or the refusal to do something.

I am a perfectionist—is that OCD?

It could be, depending on how strongly you believe you need to be perfect and what you do in order to try to be perfect. If you can do things without spending hours and hours on little details for ordinary tasks, that is not OCD. If you have a hobby and you spend hours on something related to the hobby, that is not really OCD either. But if you spend hours on everyday tasks because you would be too anxious to have them not be perfect, then that could be OCD. Or if you have a hobby, but you never actually complete anything because you can never get it to be "just right," then that could be OCD as well.

For perfectionism to meet the criteria for OCD, you would probably have obsessive thoughts telling you that you had to do things perfectly—most likely that you would not be accepted by others if you were not perfect. You would need to perform compulsive behaviors to try to get things done perfectly, even at the expense of getting those things done on time or even at the expense of your relationships with others—for example, people may get frustrated if you're constantly making them late because you can't leave the house until everything is perfect. If your OCD tells you that doing something perfectly is all that makes you acceptable to others, then angering them by doing the rituals is not important because, in your head, once you complete the task perfectly, everything will be fine. However, this is often not the case, and people with OCD focused on perfectionism often get fired from their jobs and alienate their friends and family. Unfortunately, to seek relief, they try even harder to be perfect rather than giving up their futile quest for perfection.

Is there such a thing as situational OCD—is it possible to be obsessive about only one thing?

There is no such thing as situational OCD. OCD, however, can be very specific—for example, your bathroom may be the main focus of your OCD, and other areas may not be as important. This is purely a result of your own obsessions about your bathroom versus the other rooms, even other bathrooms, in your home. If your only fear is related to the cleanliness of your bathroom, then that is all you will focus on. You may not even be concerned about any other bathroom in the house given that bathrooms you don't use will have little effect on you because nothing in there can harm you; you have no interaction with those bathrooms. However, you may have obsessions about your own bathroom and will therefore perform the compulsive cleaning to deal with the obsessions.

It is possible that no other room in the house bothers you because the bathroom is the only place where you urinate and defecate. If you see these bodily functions as dirty and somehow contaminating your bathroom, then you may want to clean your bathroom a great deal to assure that there is nothing harmful there. There are individuals with OCD who are very focused on going to the bathroom— some go so far as to wear latex gloves when they defecate or urinate, and others wipe their anus for an hour or more to be sure that there are no feces left. Although these are extreme cases, bathrooms can be the source of a great deal of anxiety for people with OCD.

It is important that treatment for anyone with bathroom fears focuses specifically on those fears. Often, when working with a person with such fears, therapists conduct therapy in a bathroom to help that person with his or her fears. The therapist and the patient may touch all of the fixtures in the bathroom or hold sink or toilet handles. Whatever the fear is, it is important for the therapist and patient to work together to overcome any OCD fears.

Do people with OCD fear bodily fluids?

Many people with OCD fear bodily fluids—it is a very prevalent obsession in OCD—and it can have a major effect on them and on their personal relationships. This fear can affect people with OCD in several ways.

First, they may fear saliva because it can carry germs from the mouth, or they may fear mucus from the nose because it can also be seen as carrying viruses. Therefore, they may refuse to shake a person's hand if they see that person blowing his or her nose or coughing into his or her hand. Although their goal is to protect themselves from getting ill, they may be perceived as rude for not shaking hands. This fear can also keep people from going out in public at all.

Conversely, people with this fear also may not want to go out in public if *they* are coughing or sneezing, so that they will not be responsible for inadvertently getting others ill. They would feel horrible if they knew they had made someone else sick, so they do not want to take the risk.

Although these fluids can be a focus of OCD, the bodily excretions that appear to cause the most problems are feces, urine, and semen. Because vaginal secretions are not often forcefully ejected from the body, they appear to be less problematic than the others.

Even though urine is sterile when it comes out of the body, many individuals with OCD spend a great deal of time washing their hands in order to remove any trace of it. Often their fear is that they will spread their urine around and somehow contaminate others. In a similar vein, there is also a fear of having feces on their hand after they wipe their anus and of then spreading it to other surfaces or individuals and contaminating them and their environment. Some individuals have gone to such extremes as to wear rubber gloves when urinating or defecating as a way to keep their hands clean, though they often still wash their hands far more than necessary after removing the gloves.

Finally, there are men who have a great deal of difficulty with semen. They fear being contaminated by touching something that may have semen on it or contaminating others if they were to accidentally spread their semen around after masturbating or having a nocturnal emission (wet dream). They may fear somehow getting a woman pregnant without knowing it. So, if a man were to have a wet dream and then not clean himself enough, he could still have semen on his body and then touch a chair. Later on that day a woman could sit in that chair, and the man may fear that he could have somehow left enough semen on the chair that it would be able to pass through her clothes, enter her vagina, and get her pregnant. These obsessions with bodily fluids are clearly illogical, but can become extremely debilitating.

I really like the Sci-Fi Channel—people say I am obsessed with it. Does this mean I have OCD?

No, this does not necessarily mean that you have OCD. When people say that they are obsessed with something like a television show, what they typically mean is that they really like it and look forward to seeing it again. They may even record it and watch it several times or go online and join a chat group about it.

In order for OCD to be involved, there has to be some type of anxiety attached to the channel. If you had to go to a wedding, you would most likely be fine and not worry about the Sci-Fi Channel, even if you forgot to record it. You might be disappointed, but that would be expected—many of us would be disappointed if we missed out on something that we really enjoy. However, if you recorded the channel every day, checked the recorder several times before leaving the house, and even came back home at lunch to be sure that the recorder was working, these might be OCD behaviors because these behaviors go beyond what we would typically see most people do. These could be compulsive behaviors all done to relieve the anxiety about missing something on the Sci-Fi Channel.

I am in high school and have a huge crush on this football player. I can't stop thinking of him—I even dream of him! Do I have OCD?

No, you have hormones. Just because you are "obsessed" with someone does not mean that you have OCD. In fact, if having a crush on someone and dreaming of him or her meant people had OCD, almost the entire population would have OCD at some point in their lives.

This is very normal behavior, especially while going through puberty. It is very common to develop very strong feelings for people very quickly, only to have them dashed a week later, and then to develop a crush on someone else the next day. This is just the way our brains and emotions work during adolescence. But this can also occur as we age. Married people may meet someone else and find it difficult to get that person out of their head.

Parents often think of their children a great deal, especially when they are newborns, but we would not label this as OCD either. Therefore, thinking of people and dreaming of them does not constitute an obsession in the OCD sense of the definition. Obsessions must be intrusive, and rarely do adolescent girls find thoughts about the star football player to be intrusive—in fact, they seem to enjoy it and tell all of their friends about it. Most people with OCD would not do that. In fact, individuals with OCD would attempt to neutralize the thoughts, and rarely does someone with a crush try to stop thinking about the object of his or her affections.

Some people wonder if OCD can lead to stalking behavior. Most likely this would not happen, for the simple reason that people with OCD do not want to get caught or draw attention to themselves. It is possible that a person may have intrusive thoughts about a person, but taking that to the much higher level of stalking goes beyond OCD and probably into the realm of a personality disorder or some type of psychotic behavior.

Do athletes have OCD when they perform good-luck rituals before each game, like drinking the same kind of soda or putting on the same dirty socks?

Possibly. It really depends on the athlete and whether they are able to play a game without doing a good-luck ritual. If the athlete one day makes a mistake and forgets to do his or her good-luck ritual and is plagued with the thought that because he or she did not do it he or she will lose the game, then there is a possibility that some OCD is occurring. However, if the person is able to realize that even though he or she did not do the good-luck ritual, he or she could still win the game, then there would be no OCD.

Many athletes develop these "lucky" rituals because they pair certain experiences or events with winning a game. So, if one morning they ate Sugarpoofs cereal and then went on to pitch a no-hitter, there is a chance they'll try to eat Sugarpoofs before they pitch their next game. Now, do Sugarpoofs have anything to do with winning a game? Of course not, but some people think that if it worked once, why take a chance and not do it the next time? So, they keep on eating Sugarpoofs. But if one day they run out of Sugarpoofs, they have a choice—they can eat another cereal, or they can go to the store and buy Sugarpoofs. This would not be OCD, but a habit. However, if they get to the store and find no Sugarpoofs, and then they either call the coach and refuse to pitch or do pitch but think only about how bad everything is going to be because they did not get to eat their Sugarpoofs, then a diagnosis of OCD is possible. These negative thoughts would most likely interfere with their pitching and concentration, likely leading them to pitch a bad game and probably to be taken out of the game very early. Of course, a thorough evaluation with a mental health professional would be necessary to actually diagnose OCD.

Many children develop certain routines or want things done in very specific ways—is this OCD or just a normal part of growing up?

This is a normal part of growing up. Children will fixate on certain things, such as a blanket or a pacifier. They may even have set patterns of saying goodnight or giving hugs and kisses. All of this is normal. It becomes a problem when a violation occurs and they are unable to handle the change in their routine. This still may not be OCD, but it may require you to do some exposures (see Chapter 7) to help your child adjust to differences in routines and to get him or her to accept that changes happen. If there are still difficulties, then consulting with a behavioral therapist may be necessary to help you come up with exercises to help your child adjust to new routines or occurrences.

What's the difference between someone with OCD and someone who just likes to be organized?

The person who merely likes to be organized prefers organization, but he or she would be able to handle disarray and not let it interfere with his or her life. The person with OCD, on the other hand, would not be able to tolerate disarray. This person would have a difficult time accomplishing anything else because of the fact that things were unorganized, and he would want to compulsively organize everything to get rid of his obsessive thoughts about disorganization.

There is nothing wrong with liking organization, and we often hear of people who like organization being called OCD. However, this is usually meant to tease people instead of being an actual diagnosis. There is nothing wrong with having preferences, as long as they do not interfere with your life or as long as you can accept that at times you will not be able to do things the way you prefer to do them. If you cannot accept that, and it would lead to great difficulties, then a diagnosis of OCD may be warranted.

What are the most common symptoms of OCD?

At the most basic level, occurrences of obsessional thoughts, impulses, or images, coupled with compulsive behaviors, are the most common symptoms of OCD. But in terms of what is observable to most people, common symptoms include, but are not limited to, compulsively performing any or all of these actions:

- Checking (for example, repeatedly making sure locks on doors and windows are fastened)
- Washing (hands, clothing, or household items)

- Praying (asking for forgiveness or a special dispensation)
- Confessing (telling others of bad thoughts so that they will confirm that you are not really bad)
- Symmetry (having to touch your left side if your right side was touched)
- Straightening (can manifest in all things being placed at 90 degree angles or similar compulsions)
- Touching (having to touch certain items in a certain order)
- Repeating (saying something over a certain number of times or doing a task a certain number of times)
- Avoiding (not going to a place where you know you will engage in compulsive behaviors, such as a public restroom)
- Reassurance-seeking (repeatedly asking others to tell you that everything is OK)

How do you tell the difference between true OCD and simple obsessive thinking?

There is no difference. If a person has obsessive thinking, then that person has OCD. Remember, you need to have only obsessions *or* compulsions for OCD, not both (though 96 percent of people with OCD have both). As long as the criteria for an obsession discussed at the beginning of the chapter are met, then the diagnosis of OCD can be met. If, however, a person just can't get a thought out of his or her head, and it is more of an annoyance than anything, this does not meet the criteria for an obsession. Almost all of us have experienced this at some time, but it does not mean that we all have OCD.

Something escalates to the realm of an obsession when it is intrusive and inappropriate, and a random thought typically does not reach that level. Further, people with OCD typically attempt to somehow neutralize an obsession, whereas individuals who experience a random thought just try to get rid of it and typically think nothing of it beyond it being a thought. Individuals with OCD give more credence to their thoughts than do people without OCD—believing that having had that thought makes them a bad person or that now that they have had that thought, it is likely to come true.

What are some typical themes of obsessions?

There are numerous core fears that you might face if you have OCD:

- **Subjugation.** This is the idea that you must sacrifice your own needs constantly for the needs of others. The only way to feel better is to be sure that everyone else is OK even if you are not.
- **Vulnerability to harm or illness.** If you have this fear, you believe that disaster can strike at any time, so being prepared—even overprepared—is the best thing.
- **Losing self-control.** This is the fear of involuntarily losing control (e.g., of thoughts, of bodily functions), which could lead you to believe that your life is unraveling.
- **Emotional deprivation.** You worry that your needs will never be met; no matter how hard you try to please others, they will never return the favor and please you enough, and you will always be miserable.
- **Abandonment.** You fear eternal isolation and the loss of people who are close to you.
- **Mistrust.** You feel that people are basically mean and want to hurt you, so you need to do all that you can to protect yourself from them.
- **Alienation.** You feel that you are different from everyone else, so you attempt to hide your differences from people so that they will not abandon you.

- **Worthiness/Social Undesirability.** You fear that you are flawed and totally unlovable, but think that if you do everything perfectly, maybe people will overlook your flaws.
- **Incompetence.** You fear that you cannot perform to high enough standards to be accepted by others.
- **Guilt.** You think you deserve punishment for the thoughts you have and the behaviors you do.
- **Dependence.** You think you cannot function without the support of others, or one person specifically.

What if someone likes the thoughts he keeps having over and over—is that OCD?

No. A hallmark of OCD is that the thoughts are intrusive, and a person must try to ignore, suppress, or neutralize them. Therefore, if you are experiencing thoughts that you enjoy, they are not OCD thoughts.

Say there are two people who have thoughts about harming someone. One person is afraid of the thoughts, they attempt to get rid of the thoughts, and they do whatever it takes to make sure that they do not do any harm to anyone. This person probably has OCD, and feels very guilty for having these thoughts. The other person enjoys the thoughts, even entertains the idea of buying a weapon, or begins to follow the person that he is thinking of harming to get to know what the person's patterns are during the day—where he works, lives, goes to eat, etc. This is not OCD—these are potentially dangerous behaviors and ought to be taken very seriously, especially if he enjoys these thoughts.

What are some examples of checking obsessions and compulsions?

Obsession	Compulsion
The garage door might spontaneously go up, and then robbers would be able to steal my dog.	Sit in the driveway for 5 minutes after the door closes to make sure that it will not go up on its own.
If I left the iron on, it might burn the house down.	Going back to the laundry room over 10 times just to be sure that the iron is unplugged and not on.
If the pilot light on the stove goes out, we could all die from a lack of oxygen.	Getting up numerous times over the course of the night to be sure that the pilot light has not blown out.
If I have a spelling error in this document, everyone will think that I am incompetent.	Running the spell check numerous times before printing out the document, reading the printout numerous times to be sure there are no errors, and, even after handing it in, asking for it back to just check it a few more times to be sure that it is error-free.

What are some examples of contamination obsessions and compulsions?

Obsession	Compulsion
If I touch that bathroom door handle, I will get HIV.	Make all attempts to avoid touching or going near the bathroom door handle, or only opening it with a towel or your sleeve.
My bowel movements are disgusting.	Taking a shower after every bowel movement to be sure that there is no feces on your body.
People who work in hospitals are full of germs.	Not going within half of a mile of a hospital or medical center, or not shopping or eating near one, in case any of the employees have been there and have spread their germs.
My child is very susceptible to germs.	Washing all of your child's toys with alcohol on a daily basis for several hours to be sure they are free of any germs.

What are some examples of hoarding obsessions and compulsions?

Obsession	Compulsions
That spatula is on sale for only 99 cents, so I should buy it.	Buying the spatula because it is such a good bargain, even though you already have twelve spatulas.

Obsession	Compulsion
That microwave on the side of the road could be repaired.	Pulling over and picking up the microwave, even though you already have fifteen broken microwaves at your home that you hope to fix.
If I were to lose this item, then I would lose the ability to access the memories that I associate with it.	You have to keep all of your children's clothes from grade school, even though they are in college, because seeing their clothes is all you have to remind you of when they were younger.
If I do not take care of these stray animals, no one will, and they will die.	Your house is overrun with all kinds of animals.

What are some examples of symmetry obsessions and compulsions?

Obsession	Compulsion
That picture on the wall is going to drive me crazy if it is not straight.	Going and straightening a picture, even if it is not yours or it is not an opportune time to do it (such as in the middle of a meeting).
Someone bumped me on my left side, and now things are uneven.	Following that person and bumping into him or her on the right side to make things even.

Obsession	Compulsion
I have to make an equal number of left and right turns on my way home, or something bad might happen.	Going out of your way on the way home in order to get in an equal number of turns.
I cannot work unless I straighten up my desk, because all I will think about is my messy desk.	Straightening your desk for several hours each day at the expense of your work productivity.

What are some examples of scrupulosity obsessions and compulsions?

Obsession	Compulsion
Because Jesus has only a loincloth on while hanging on the cross, I keep thinking of him naked.	You say a certain number of prayers each day to ask for forgiveness for this thought.
I may have committed an unpardonable sin.	You feel you must ask God to forgive you for committing the unpardonable sin and hope that He will make an exception in your case.
What if I really wanted to worship Satan instead of God?	You have to go to confession every day to be sure that a priest will forgive you for wanting to worship Satan.
If I turn my back to the Bible, God will think I am turning away from him or mooning him.	You sleep facing the Bible, and if you wake up facing away from it, you have to ask God for his forgiveness.

What are some examples of harm obsessions?

Obsession	Compulsion
If my daughter sits on my lap, I might molest her.	You do not let your daughter sit on your lap anymore, even when she asks to.
If I use sharp objects in the kitchen, I might stab someone that walks by me.	You no longer cut things with anything sharper than a butter knife.
If I see a bicyclist while I am driving, I might want to hit him.	You refuse to drive anymore, only allowing yourself to take public transportation.
If I don't count up to a certain number, I might be the cause of a natural disaster.	You constantly count in your head to ward off major disasters you think you may be responsible for.

Do people with OCD really have control over their disorder but just do it to get attention?

An untreated sufferer has very little control over his or her OCD—however, it is not a question of control as much as it is a question of fear. Once people with OCD learn how to handle their fear, they can often see improvements in their OCD. If people with OCD had no control over their disorder, then even therapy would not be helpful.

As for attention, therapists have found that people with OCD often do not want attention drawn to them; they prefer to do their rituals in private or with little fanfare. If people really wanted to get attention, there are better ways to get it than to have OCD.

Chapter 3

CAUSES OF OCD

- Why do people develop OCD?
- Do people with OCD have a chemical imbalance?
- Does OCD stem from a serious unconscious psychological problem?
- What increases my risk for OCD?
- How is avoidance of what you fear related to OCD?
- How is reassurance-seeking related to OCD?
- Is OCD a punishment from a god?
- Can I catch OCD from someone?
- Is OCD the result of a moral or ethical problem?
- I heard that OCD and strep throat might be related to each other (PANDAS). Is that true?
- If my child develops PANDAS, what course of treatment will we need to take?
- Can you acquire OCD gradually, or do you just get it?
- Is OCD the result of nature or nurture, or is it a result of a combination of both?
- Did I give OCD to my child?
- Does OCD have anything to do with the fight or flight response?
- Will we ever definitely know the cause of OCD?
- Do diet and exercise have any effect on OCD?

Why do people develop OCD?

The response to this question may depend on who is answering it. A therapist who specializes in Cognitive Behavioral Therapy (CBT) may say that OCD is a result of the belief that an intrusive thought, impulse, or image and the resulting anxiety that is generated need to be neutralized, or else the thought will somehow come true, or a dire consequence will occur. The relief that occurs after performing the compulsion feels very good to the person, but at the same time it is the beginning of a pattern of behavior that will increase over time— now that the person has learned a way to rid him- or herself of the obsession, he or she will be more likely to repeat the behavior the next time the obsessive thought occurs.

A psychiatrist may say that a person with OCD is experiencing a chemical imbalance. This is based on previous findings that have shown that certain medications, such as selective serotonin reuptake inhibitors (SSRIs), lead to an increase of serotonin in the brain and a decrease in OCD behaviors for some patients (see Chapter 8 for more information on medicating OCD). Therefore, with the right combination of medications, psychiatrists believe OCD will decrease over time as the chemicals become balanced.

A neuroimaging researcher may say that OCD is the result of abnormalities in the physical structure of the brain. Neuroimages of the brain (such as PET scans, MRIs, etc.) show what areas are working, or "firing," while a person is focusing on an obsession or performing a compulsion. These images are compared with images of the brain functions of people who do not have OCD and who are thinking the same thoughts or performing the same behaviors. A neuroimager is looking for differences between these two groups in how the brain functions, and then they form hypotheses about how disorders develop based on the differences they find.

It is probable that OCD develops because of a combination of all of these factors. More research is needed to say for sure how each one of these areas interact with and influence the others.

Do people with OCD have a chemical imbalance?

As stated in the previous answer, the idea of a neurological chemical imbalance being a cause of OCD came from research that showed that certain medications have an effect on OCD. Therefore, it stands to reason that the medications brought the chemicals in the person's brain back into a balance.

There are some problems with this reasoning, however. First, this assumes that people are born with a perfect balance of chemicals in their brain. The changes that children undergo through their first years of life are monumental. As they grow and interact with their environment, huge changes occur in the form and function of their brain, even at the neurotransmitter level (neurotransmitters are the chemical messengers in the brain that are supposedly in or out of balance). Neurotransmitters are the brain's means of communication because the neurons (brain cells) in your brain are not actually connected to each other. Instead, there is a small space between them—in order to communicate, they send messages back and forth using neurotransmitters. Therefore, if chemical balance is the goal, we should be medicating all newborns to prevent such dramatic changes in brain functioning and chemistry. However, if we were to do this, then we would not develop appropriately—drugging all our newborns is obviously not a viable option.

An obvious solution to this is waiting until the brain is fully formed before trying to establish a balance. However, there is a problem with this as well. A neurological chemical balance is unique to each person—even though all of our brains have a similar physical and chemical makeup, they function a bit differently based on who we are as individuals. So there is no balance to be had that will work for everyone.

Medications for OCD affect the transmission of the neurotransmitters, increasing them or decreasing them to bring about "optimal" levels. However, people do not often stay at one dose of medicine for their whole lives. Changes occur, depending on events in a person's life. Or some people successfully go off of medications for years, but then have a relapse. This would mean that medications brought them into balance and that balance was maintained for years without medications but was then lost, and medications had to be reintroduced to return the balance.

Jon Abromowitz put it best in his book *Understanding and Treating Obsessive-Compulsive Disorder* (2006) with this example: "When I take aspirin, my headache goes away. Thus, the reason I get headaches is because my aspirin level is too low." No one would believe that they have a low aspirin level and that they need to bring that level back into balance. In a similar vein, there are many ways that neurotransmitters work and are involved in the development and maintenance of OCD. To suggest that we are somehow out of balance, though, does not appear to be a worthwhile or meaningful explanation.

Does OCD stem from a serious unconscious psychological problem?

OCD need not stem from a serious unconscious psychological problem; in fact, OCD is a serious psychological problem on its own. There are numerous theories as to why OCD develops—some with more merit than others—but the idea that someone is manifesting OCD symptoms as a result of a serious unconscious problem is very much "old school" psychology. Explanations such as conflict with your mother while toilet training or secretly lusting after her are outdated. Although there may still be a few therapists who believe that these reasons are valid, the majority of people in the field will say that the current cognitive, behavioral, or neuro-chemical theories (see "Why do people develop OCD?" on page 48) are far better at explaining OCD. The therapies being used today are based on these newer theories and have brought about great relief of OCD symptoms.

What increases my risk for OCD?

There is no single answer to this question. It appears that your risks for OCD are increased if you have a family member with OCD, if you have some of the chromosomal markers for the disorder, if you have certain abnormalities in specific parts of your brain, and if you react to intrusive thoughts, images, or impulses in such a way that you believe having these thoughts, impulses, or images can somehow make them come true. These are probably the greatest risk factors for OCD.

Other risk factors may be experiencing a traumatic event, being highly religious, having a newborn baby in the immediate family, and the influence of culture (Japanese individuals are very concerned about offending others with their personal odor, for example).

Whatever the risk factors, just because you have a risk factor does not mean that you will develop OCD, and just because you cannot identify any risk factors does not mean that you will never have OCD. There is still much for us to learn about how we develop and maintain mental disorders.

How is avoidance of what you fear related to OCD?

Not only is this related to OCD; it may very well be the essential behavior that prolongs the existence of OCD. Basically, it comes down to this—the more you avoid what you are afraid of, the more you teach yourself that the only way to be safe is to continue to avoid it. Therefore, avoidance begets more avoidance. As avoidance behaviors are allowed to continue unchecked, they will lead to more and more rituals, as well as possibly more involved rituals, such as adding more steps to the ritual or having to do the ritual for longer and longer periods of time to reach the desired calm.

Eliminating the avoidance of your fears is the focus of exposure therapy—you are gradually reintroduced to the objects or situations you have been avoiding. This therapy is designed to get people to go back to doing the things that the obsessions tell them are dangerous so that they can see that just thinking something does not mean it is true or has a greater chance of becoming real.

How is reassurance-seeking related to OCD?

The more you seek reassurance, the more you will want it. Reassurance is, in many ways, like a drug. People who take drugs need more and more of that drug over time to get the same high. In a similar vein, people who seek reassurance want more and more reassurance as time goes on. What you gave them in the form of reassurance yesterday will not be enough today.

Also, people use reassurance to help them put off an unwanted consequence. A drug user who is going through withdrawal wants the drug to stop the withdrawal symptoms, just like someone with OCD wants reassurance that everything will be OK so that he or she can break free of the discomfort of the obsession. The problem is that if you give the drug user the drug to stop the withdrawal, you are effectively maintaining the addiction. The same can be said for OCD. If you receive reassurance to alleviate the discomfort caused by the obsession, then you never learn that you can handle the obsession without getting the reassurance, and the OCD is maintained and even strengthened.

As with the issue of avoidance, exposure and response prevention (ERP) is a therapy that can help to eliminate reassurance-seeking. A therapist has people with OCD confront what they fear without giving them a great deal of reassurance. As time goes on, the giving of reassurance is eliminated, and the people in therapy learn that they can handle their fears on their own without needing assistance from others. (See page 131 for more information on ERP.)

Is OCD a punishment from a god?

The answer to this question will depend on who is answering. There are some people who would say that OCD is a punishment from a higher power, and they may suggest some spiritual type of healing as a cure. Others may say that OCD is the result of what has already been discussed in the book, such as intrusive thoughts, neurochemicals, or even strep throat. Either way, only the research that we have discussed in this book is testable, so we can never answer the question of whether OCD could be a punishment from a higher power because we can never test that.

However, whether OCD is a punishment from a god is not as important as what you are going to do about your OCD. There is a joke about a guy who is in a flood. An evacuation squad pulls up to his door in a truck and tells him he must leave, or he may die in the flood. He responds, "No, God will save me." Later, a boat comes up to his window, and the evacuation squad tells him to get in. He replies again, "No, God will save me." Finally, he is on the roof of his home, surrounded by water, and a helicopter comes along. A ladder is dropped and the evacuation squad tells him to climb the ladder, and he yells, "No, God will save me!" Minutes later, he drowns in the flood. Upon entering heaven, he demands to talk to God. He is granted his request, and he angrily yells at God, "I prayed and prayed for you to save me, and you let me die!" God looks at him and says, "I sent a truck, a boat, and a helicopter—what more did you want?"

The point is, no matter what the cause, there is treatment available to assist you—you may just need to look for it.

Can I catch OCD from someone?

No. OCD is not a communicable disease; it is a disorder, which means it develops based on how an individual's brain processes the information from his or her environment and that individual's resulting actions. Someone without OCD may touch a garbage can and think nothing of it, whereas someone with OCD may touch it and fear being contaminated to the point of obsession. OCD is not caught from someone else, but develops based on a person's own thoughts, feelings, behaviors, and brain chemistry.

Some research indicates that OCD may be related, in a very small number of cases, to strep throat infections, which you can catch from someone else, but there would be no way in that situation to say that someone caused OCD in another person. It would be the result of the infection. (See "I heard that OCD and strep throat might be related to each other (PANDAS). Is that true?" on page 55 for more information on strep throat and OCD.) And, while there are genetic links in OCD, they are not 100 percent, so we cannot say for sure that, for instance, a child "catches" OCD from her parent.

Is OCD the result of a moral or ethical problem?

No research indicates that OCD is the result of a moral or ethical problem, nor is there any way to prove this using science. Science is based on observable and testable facts and experiments. Because we cannot investigate or observe a moral problem, we cannot make an inference that a moral problem is the cause of OCD.

What we can say about morality and OCD is that, at times, OCD can focus on morals or ethics. Some people with OCD fear doing things that are morally or ethically wrong. Some fear offending a higher power, and others are afraid that they will be damned or seen as evil people for their thoughts or actions. Therefore, it is easy for these people to infer that OCD might be related to moral or ethical problems. However, this is just the effect of the OCD obsession with morality; for as many people who have moral or ethical issues related to their OCD, there are even more that have no moral or ethical association with their OCD whatsoever. If OCD were the result of a moral or ethical problem, then all people with OCD would be focused on moral and ethical matters.

I heard that OCD and strep throat might be related to each other (PANDAS). Is that true?

There is some research suggesting that strep throat infections may result in the development of antibodies that, in some children, actually attack the basal ganglia in the brain (an area associated with the development of OCD). When this occurs, OCD symptoms may develop. This is referred to as PANDAS, or pediatric autoimmune neuropsychiatric disorders associated with strep. This is most common in prepubescent children.

Differentiating between the development of OCD from PANDAS and how it usually develops is not difficult if you know what to look for. Although OCD typically develops over the course of months or years, PANDAS is rapid in onset, with some parents saying that one day their children were fine, and the next day they had OCD. This is the main indicator of PANDAS. Other indicators in children may be the rapid development of tics, acting infantile or much younger than they actually are, or separation anxiety.

In order to conclusively diagnose PANDAS, it is important to get a strep throat culture to assess the presence of group A beta-hemolytic streptococcal infection, or to get blood work done to check for the level of strep-related titers in the blood. In relation to PANDAS, titers are a measure of the level of certain antibodies in the blood. Normal levels of these titers are 200–300, whereas many individuals with PANDAS OCD will have blood titer levels 500-700 and above.

Successful treatment of PANDAS is dual—you need to eliminate both the underlying strep infection and the OCD symptoms.

If my child develops PANDAS, what course of treatment will we need to take?

If your child develops PANDAS, start him or her on a dose of antibiotics that is strong enough to deal with the underlying infection. This may require a few rounds of medication and several blood draws to be sure that the infection has been neutralized.

At the same time, it will be important to start an aggressive treatment program of exposure and response prevention (ERP). Just because the infection is cleared up does not mean that the OCD will be gone—it may be easier to treat, but it can still be there. Therefore, it will be important to do the therapy until the child's behavior returns to what it was before the infection.

Can you acquire OCD gradually, or do you just get it?

The only way to really develop OCD quickly is to acquire it because of PANDAS (see the previous two questions and answers). Otherwise, OCD tends to develop gradually over the course of months or years. However, certain traumatic events may quicken the development of OCD. For example, if a person is worried about being fired and therefore attempts to do everything perfectly, but he gets fired anyway because of cutbacks and not because of anything related to his performance, he may still blame himself for not being perfect enough. This could increase the symptoms of his OCD, and his perfectionism could jump out of control.

Often, individuals attempt to hide their OCD until it is very difficult to fight and becomes apparent to others. This is unfortunate, as early therapy can be very helpful. Once others notice the symptoms, it may appear as if there was a rapid onset, but the sufferer may have just been hiding or masking her OCD for years.

Is OCD the result of nature or nurture, or is it a result of a combination of both?

The prevailing theory is that it is a combination of both. Although the psychological bases for OCD have been well noted in the research literature, recent DNA investigations have led to new areas of study. Researchers have discovered possible genetic markers for OCD on chromosomes 1, 3, 7, 6, and 15. The study of these markers, however, will involve years of investigation before anyone can state definitively the role of genes in the development of OCD.

In the combination of nature and nurture, the nature part has to do with our genetic and biological makeup. We all have certain genetic predispositions toward specific things. Our family history creates susceptibility for certain diseases or disorders in our genetic code. However, just because we may have a susceptibility does not mean that we will develop a disorder. That is where the nurture part of the combination occurs. We need to have the right stressors at the right times in order to "kick off" the predispositions that we have.

If OCD were influenced purely by our genetics, then every time one identical twin developed OCD, the other twin would have OCD as well. However, this does not happen. Although the prevalence of both twins having OCD if one twin has it is high (potentially 65—85 percent), it is not 100 percent, therefore suggesting that nurture or other environmental triggers have some type of influence on the development of OCD.

For example, assume that there are identical twins with a genetic predisposition toward OCD. If they are adopted apart at birth, and one of them develops OCD, and the other does not, we can say that the environment played a major role because that is the only difference between the two twins, who are genetically identical.

Did I give OCD to my child?

You did not give OCD to your child. You may have, however, passed on a susceptibility for OCD to your child. Scientifically determining how disorders may be transmitted genetically is still in its infancy, but some findings suggest that children born to parents who have OCD may be at a higher risk for developing OCD than children born to parents without it. In fact, if anyone in your immediate family has OCD, your chance of having it is about 20 percent, versus around 2.5 percent in the general population.

However, an environmental aspect may be at play here as well. It is possible that the children of parents with OCD are influenced by their environment, which encourages the development of OCD behaviors. Yet if this was the only factor, then these children would most likely have the same obsessions and compulsions as their parents, but this is rare. Therefore, the combination of the genetic contributions of the parents and the environment in which the child lives both play a role in the development of OCD.

There is also a hidden meaning in this question: "Is it my fault that my child has OCD?" The answer to this would be no, unless you purposely wanted your child to have OCD, and we are not aware of any parents who would wish this on their children. Parents generally try to do what they feel is best for their children, but this can backfire with OCD. For example, a mother who cleans all of her children's toys with rubbing alcohol for hours each day is attempting to prevent her children from becoming contaminated by germs. Although the intention is admirable, the action is compulsive, and the children will, most likely, learn more from their mother about cleaning than about her hope that they will be germ-free. Over time, her behavior has a good chance of influencing them in establishing their own compulsive behaviors.

Does OCD have anything to do with the fight or flight response?

Absolutely. The intrusive and obsessive thoughts, impulses, or images that characterize OCD create fear in you, and that fear elicits a fight or flight response. It is actually called the Fight/Flight/Freeze (FFF) response, because you may have three reactions to a stressor—you will either (a) fight it off, (b) run away from it, or (c) freeze and hope it passes by you without it noticing you. The compulsion that is performed to neutralize the obsession is a way of "flight" from the fear of the obsession. The compulsion removes the feared effects of the obsession, and the person experiences relief. However, that relief is only temporary, and the obsession returns again and again, leading to more compulsive behavior. Exposure therapy (which we discuss more in Chapter 7) relies on choosing the fight response—that is, facing the feared obsession without performing a compulsion and learning that you can handle the outcome.

Will we ever definitely know the cause of OCD?

It is easy to see why people would want an answer to "why." In our society, we can go to the doctor to get medication or surgery for numerous problems that afflict us. If we have an infection, we take an antibiotic. If we have a tumor, we remove it and follow that with radiation and chemotherapy. If we have a headache, we take a pain reliever, and the pain subsides. Further, we can attribute a cause to many of these problems, such as bacteria causing an infection, smoking leading to the development of a lung cancer, and a head injury leading to a headache.

With mental disorders, we cannot be that precise because the brain is the most complex thing in the known universe. We are just beginning to understand how it works and functions. We are nowhere near the level of sophistication of being able to say that one experience led to the development of a disorder. The reason for this is simple—if an environmental experience did lead to the development of a disorder, then every person that experienced that environment would develop the disorder, and this simply does not happen. Therefore, it is the interaction of our environment and our brain (back to nature and nurture) that leads to the development of disorders, and therefore to OCD. Can specific experiences lead to the development of OCD in a specific person? Of course, but is that experience going to lead to the development of OCD in every person? No.

Do diet and exercise have any effect on OCD?

Diet and exercise can have an effect on everything in our life, from our physical health to our mental health. Therefore, it is important to consider these areas as you are developing a treatment plan for your OCD.

We know that exercise can have a positive effect on serotonin, one of the neurotransmitters thought to be related to OCD. This effect on serotonin could in turn lead to a positive effect on your OCD as well, given that regulation of serotonin is one of the things that psychiatrists hope to do when prescribing medications to treat OCD.

There are some indications that diet also may affect OCD. In the past, there were some attempts to treat OCD with tryptophan, one of the sources for the building blocks of the neurotransmitters related to OCD. However, tryptophan is currently banned by the Food and Drug Administration (FDA) in pure form, so the only way to get it is through foods, such as turkey or kiwi fruit. Other researchers have looked into using B6 vitamin therapy because B6 is required to break tryptophan down into the base chemicals that are the building blocks of neurotransmitters. But as long as tryptophan is banned, it is impossible to continue to study its effects on OCD.

Other chemicals in our foods can have a direct impact on our level of anxiety. For example, caffeine, because it is a stimulant, can lead to a heightened level of anxiety. And vitamins and minerals, such as iron, B vitamins, calcium, phosphorous, and potassium, have been linked to decreasing stress and anxiety.

Eating habits can also be indicative of anxiety. Some people are nervous eaters and use food to try to calm themselves, typically eating carbohydrates (comfort food). The problem with this is that when people eat a large amount of carbohydrates, their serotonin levels rise, and they feel euphoric. This does not last very long, however, and then they crash, and serotonin levels dip even lower than they were before the person ate the carbohydrates. This can lead to a desire to eat even more carbohydrates, and a cycle of nervous eating can begin. With this comes weight gain, more stress, and more difficulties with mood regulation. People with OCD need to be careful about not falling victim to this pattern of self-medicating with food.

Chapter 4

OBSESSIONS

- How much time per day do people with OCD typically spend obsessing?
- Why can't I be 100 percent sure that an obsessive impulse will not come into my head again?
- Why do I have these thoughts when I don't want to?
- I have bad thoughts, and I fear that I will be punished for them. What can I do to stop these thoughts?
- What are the differences between my regular thoughts and my OCD thoughts?
- I believe there are things that I should just not think—can I hold on to these beliefs but still be successfully treated for OCD?
- Does having these obsessive thoughts make me a bad person?
- I have worries that I might harm someone even though I do not want to harm that person. Will having these thoughts make me harm someone or make me more likely to harm someone?
- Is there a way to stop the obsessive thoughts from entering my head?
- If you have obsessive thoughts, will you automatically act on them?
- I really do think that it would be fine for anyone else to do _____, but if I did _____, bad things would happen to me or my loved ones— why is that?
- My obsessive thoughts are about religion. Is that common?
- Do some people have obsessions about their sexuality?
- Why did my OCD choose _____ as my obsessive thought?
- Does everyone have obsessive thoughts?
- Why does my obsession come back so fast after I complete my rituals?
- What is the difference between a superstition and OCD?

How much time per day do people with OCD typically spend obsessing?

There is no set answer to that question. The *DSM-IV-TR* (2000) says that to be diagnosed with OCD, a person must have obsessions or compulsions that last more than an hour a day, that are significantly distressing, or that significantly interfere with daily functioning. Therefore, even if a person spent less than an hour obsessing each day, the obsessions could still be so distressing that they would meet the diagnostic criteria. Or, a person may obsess for several hours a day.

There really is, however, no typical amount of obsessing. Each person is unique in the way he or she is affected by his or her obsessions. Further, there may be some days where a person obsesses very little, but then the person may spend entire days obsessing at other times.

Why can't I be 100 percent sure that an obsessive impulse will not come into my head again?

There is no such thing as 100 percent assurance about anything. There is not even 100 percent assurance that the sun will rise tomorrow—it is possible that a huge asteroid could hit the planet this evening and destroy it, meaning that there is no tomorrow. Yet most people do not worry about this, and they accept that there is always the possibility that something bad might happen. But when it comes to OCD, people want 100 percent assurance that the thing they most fear will not happen. They want to know for sure that there is no chance that they will have to deal with the obsession or perform the compulsive behavior again. It is this reassurance-seeking that often prolongs a person's struggle with OCD. As you ask more "what if" questions, your mind goes further and further into worst-case scenarios, and you actually obsess *more* about what you fear, rather than less. There is no 100 percent ability to get rid of your OCD; it is a treatable disorder, and you must always be working to fight it.

Why do I have these thoughts when I don't want to?

To get to the base of it, that really is the definition of an obsession— an intrusive and inappropriate thought, impulse, or image. Intrusive, as applied to OCD, basically means that the thought, impulse, or image occurs when you really do not want it to. Therefore, these thoughts, impulses, or images are occurring because you have OCD. It is similar to having muscle pain because you have a pulled muscle. The reason for the pain is the pulled muscle, and until that pulled muscle is repaired or allowed to heal, there will be pain. Similarly, until you get some treatment for your OCD, you will experience the unwanted thoughts, impulses, or images because the nature of OCD is to cause unwanted thoughts, images, or impulses.

I have bad thoughts, and I fear that I will be punished for them. What can I do to stop these thoughts?

First, let's address the idea that you are having bad thoughts. There are no such things as bad thoughts—there are just thoughts. Just because you think a thought is bad does not mean that it is. Further, your belief that you are having bad thoughts is likely to actually increase your OCD behaviors.

Second, how can you be punished for your thoughts? The only way that could happen is if you believed that a higher power was going to punish you. No other person can hear your thoughts, so no one can punish you for them. And if you do believe that a higher power will punish you for those bad thoughts, then why is that higher power not punishing all sorts of other people who have gotten away with cheating and lying and harming others? Here is another way to look at this: Do you believe that this higher power is all-powerful (probably, if you believe they can read your mind)? If so, then don't you think that this higher power knows that you have OCD and that it is the OCD that is leading you to have the thoughts that you are having? If that is the case, then why would that higher power punish you for what your OCD is doing?

In terms of stopping the thoughts, thoughts will always randomly pop into your head. This is human nature. The trick to stopping them is to not try to stop them. You need to recognize that because these are just thoughts, they will come and go throughout the day. If you can let them go, then you will not need to do any compulsive behaviors to try to get rid of them. And if you can refrain from compulsions, you eliminate the majority of your OCD. If you can continue to resist performing compulsions, you may realize that the themes or fears in the obsessions do not come true, even if you don't engage in the compulsions. Thus, you will become less afraid of the obsessions and will see a decrease in them as well. Of course this is a simplified version of what would happen in therapy, but the basic idea is there. Fighting thoughts just makes them stronger and last longer, whereas accepting them and testing whether the feared results do happen when you do not perform the compulsions will most likely bring a great deal of relief.

What are the differences between my regular thoughts and my OCD thoughts?

The basic difference between "regular" thoughts and OCD thoughts are that OCD thoughts are unwanted and seen as inappropriate. In addition, they cause significant anxiety and distress. Non-OCD thoughts rarely cause these results. At times, some people may experience thoughts that meet a part of the obsession definition, but that does not necessarily mean that they have OCD. If a person has suicidal thoughts, he or she may see those thoughts as unwanted and inappropriate and be very distressed by them. But these are not necessarily OCD thoughts. To diagnose a person with OCD, professionals will also look to see that the thoughts are not about real life problems, that the person tries to somehow suppress or neutralize the thoughts, and that the person recognizes that the thoughts are a product of his or her own mind. If the suicidal thought is a response to a difficult situation, then it is a concern about a real life problem, so it is not OCD. However, some people have intrusive suicidal thoughts that are not related to any real life problems. They may try to suppress or neutralize them, and they may recognize that the thoughts are a product of their own mind. In this situation, OCD could be diagnosed, given that all four criteria for an obsession are met.

I believe there are things that I should just not think—can I hold on to these beliefs but still be successfully treated for OCD?

It will be very difficult for you to achieve a full recovery from your OCD if you really do believe that there are things that you should not think. There are two reasons for this:

1. The idea that you should not think something is just an opinion. Just because you think you should not think something does not mean that anyone else would agree with you. In fact, a therapist will probably want you to think the very things you do not want to think of because this is actually very therapeutic. One of the best tools for fighting OCD is doing the very opposite of what the disorder tells you to do.
2. As we have discussed previously, there is no such thing as a bad thought. A thought is just a thought. We are not judged by our private thoughts; we are judged by our actions and our intent.

So, even if you think that a loved one will be harmed tonight, that thought does not cause the harm to happen. You do not have an intent to harm anyone, and thinking it does not somehow set into motion that process.

Holding the belief that there are thoughts that you just should not have perpetuates your OCD. It gets you to continue to believe that there is something wrong with the way you think about things, and what therapists try to do in therapy is help people counteract that belief and teach people how to let their thought processes flow naturally.

Does having these obsessive thoughts make me a bad person?

The easiest way to answer this is to ask yourself a very simple question: if your best friend had OCD, would you blame him or her for having the thoughts that you are blaming yourself for? Hopefully you answered this question with a resounding no, and if you did, then why would you blame yourself for having obsessive thoughts if you would not blame anyone else for having the same thoughts? You may think that you need to be stronger than everyone else or that you are weak because you have OCD, but you would probably not say those same things about a best friend who had OCD. So treat yourself like you were your best friend and recognize that these thoughts are related to OCD, not to you as a person. Then once you stop beating yourself up over having these OCD thoughts, you will find that you will have greater strength to fight the thoughts or to engage in therapy.

I have worries that I might harm someone even though I do not want to harm that person. Will having these thoughts make me harm someone or make me more likely to harm someone?

No, these thoughts will not make you more likely to harm someone; just because you think something does not actually mean you will do it.

A few years ago, there was an OCD patient who had a fear that he would push people into a train, so he avoided train platforms. He did not *want* to push people into trains; he just had a fear that he might accidentally do it. So he and his therapist walked down the block from her office and stood by the train tracks. When they saw that a train was coming, the therapist stood two feet from the track and had the patient stand behind her. When the train came, the therapist had the man put his hands on her shoulders and then told the man to push her as hard as he could into the train. The patient said that he would not do it, and the therapist told him repeatedly to just push her. The man refused each time. Finally, the therapist turned around and said to him, "Do you now see that you are afraid of a thought and not of a behavior?"

Is there a way to stop the obsessive thoughts from entering my head?

The best way to stop a thought from entering your head is to stop telling yourself not to think of something, or to not fight the thought when it does come into your head. If you keep telling yourself not to think of something, you are pretty much guaranteeing that you will think of it over and over.

Let's try an example—don't think of a pink elephant. Think of anything but a pink elephant, but *please* do not think about pink elephants at all.

I bet you thought of a pink elephant, or you will soon. The reason for this is the more we tell ourselves not to think of something, the more we actually think of it—we cannot help but have the thought we are trying to avoid.

To stop the thought, you need to actually think of it on purpose and sit with it. Once you realize that it is just a thought and that having it does not actually make anything bad happen, then you will be able to handle the thought.

So, try this example—think of a pink elephant. Do not think of anything other than a pink elephant. Have no thoughts of what to make for dinner, the name of your best friend in grade school, or what book to read before you go to bed. Only think of a pink elephant.

I bet you thought of the other things. Why? Because that is just how our brains work. So try to stop fighting the obsessive thoughts and just see them as what they are—thoughts and nothing more.

If you have obsessive thoughts, will you automatically act on them?

No, just because you have a thought does not mean that you will automatically act on it. If that were the case, most of us would be in jail by now. Most of us have been in a grocery store and heard a kid throwing a tantrum and wanted to go over and tell him to just shut his mouth. Or many of us have driven on a bridge and thought to ourselves, "What would happen if I just turned the wheel really sharp into the guard rail?" But, we don't do it—instead, we just have the thought and go on with our shopping or driving. The same thing happens with an obsessive thought—just because we have the thought does not mean that we will act on it.

Everyone experiences intrusive thoughts. People with OCD just happen to have a worse reaction to them than most other people do, and they get the notion that they need to do something about the thought or it will come true. People without OCD can shrug the thought off and go on with their day.

I really do think that it would be fine for anyone else to do _____, but if I did _____, bad things would happen to me or my loved ones—why is that?

This is one of the hallmarks of OCD—the idea that it would be fine for other people to do something, but that for some reason you are different, as if the rules of the world apply to you differently than they do to the other 6 billion people who live on the planet. Therefore, people with OCD are often amazed or shocked to see others not straighten things, or not wash their hands after touching doorknobs, or use a saltshaker at a restaurant that other people have touched. Although they do not necessarily think that anyone else would be harmed by doing, or not doing, any of these activities, they do believe that their own chances of being harmed are almost definite. Therefore, they avoid these activities, and because no harm befalls them when they avoid these things, they get a false sense of security in thinking that it was the avoidance that kept them safe instead of recognizing the very small probability of anything actually happening to them at all.

My obsessive thoughts are about religion. Is that common?

The main focus of OCD can be religion, especially for individuals from very fundamentalist backgrounds or for people with religions that have a lot of rules and rituals, such as Catholicism. Religiously focused OCD is actually common enough that it has earned its own subcategory from professionals: scrupulosity, from the root word "scruple," which means to show reluctance based on conscience.

Individuals with scrupulosity are often plagued with the idea that they have offended their god and will face eternal damnation if they do not somehow make amends for their transgressions. Or they fear that they are damned and that there is nothing that they can do about it, though they keep trying to figure out something to help their fate. This is similar to the mythical story of Sisyphus, who was condemned by Zeus to roll a large marble boulder up a hill, only to see it fall back to the bottom just as he was about to get it to the top. Though he knew that it was going to fall, he was condemned to do this for all eternity.

Individuals with scrupulosity often feel like Sisyphus, in that they are condemned by their OCD to a life of obsessions and compulsions. They are disgusted with themselves for having the OCD thoughts, and then they become angry at their god for their having OCD, and they then fear that they have offended their god even more for being angry at him or her, and so on. Luckily, a treatment called Cognitive Behavioral Therapy (CBT) works very well for scrupulosity. We discuss CBT in Chapter 7.

Do some people have obsessions about their sexuality?

Yes, questioning one's sexuality can be a theme in OCD. It may take several forms, such as heterosexual individuals having obsessions about being gay, homosexual individuals having obsessions about being straight, or thoughts about other sexual themes, such as sex with inanimate objects or with animals or pets. The defining characteristic of OCD with these themes is that the thoughts are unwanted versus desired or even sought after. Also, for individuals with OCD, compulsions are done to neutralize the thoughts, instead of actively seeking out encounters with the objects or people or animals in the thoughts.

Note that the thoughts about sexual orientation need not imply that there is anything wrong with being hetero or homosexual. Instead, the obsessions have to do with the perceived undesirability of either having the thoughts or of being gay or straight for that person.

Why did my OCD choose _____ as my obsessive thought?

Why OCD seems to focus on one area and not others is not totally understood. However, it appears that OCD focuses on the things that people are most afraid of. For example, a person with a contamination fear who washes her hands 50 times a day may have no fear of someone breaking into her home, so she doesn't compulsively check her locks. Yet a person with a fear of burglaries may check his locks 50 times a day and hardly ever wash his hands.

The fear on which a person with OCD is focused will be the one that is most pronounced in that person's compulsions. Maybe the person with contamination fears was once very ill and does not want that to happen again, yet her home has never been broken into, whereas the lock checker may never have been seriously ill but has had his home broken into on several occasions. Therefore, their life events have contributed to their fears.

It is also possible that no major events have happened in the lives of these individuals, but they once experienced an intrusive thought about the mere possibility of something bad happening to them in these areas, and that was enough to set off the obsessive thoughts and compulsive behaviors that they experience.

Does everyone have obsessive thoughts?

No, only people with OCD have obsessive thoughts. However, everybody does have intrusive thoughts, or thoughts that randomly pop into their head. Most people are able to shrug them off, but people with OCD do not. Instead, they attempt to ignore, suppress, or somehow neutralize the thoughts. They may tell themselves to never think that thought again, or they may attempt to replace the "bad" thought with a "good" thought. These activities are the beginnings of obsessive thinking. The more that thought suppression or neutralization is attempted, the more likely the person will develop OCD.

Why does my obsession come back so fast after I complete my rituals?

The relief that you get from the rituals is only temporary. A ritual typically relieves only one thought, impulse, or image. A minority of people with OCD can do a ritual once a day and convince themselves that this will cover them for the entire day, but that is not common. Usually, a ritual undoes one specific thought, impulse, or image and then has to be performed again when that thought, impulse, or image returns.

Because of the nature of OCD, the obsessions are intrusive, so they just keep coming back throughout the course of a day. If the rituals really worked to get rid of an obsession, then they would have to be performed only once; but the relief is only temporary, and the obsessions continue to return again and again.

The best way to get the obsession to stop returning is to stop doing the ritual and test whether the feared consequence really happens. When you realize that it doesn't, you weaken the obsession, which will lessen the recurrence of the thought, leading to fewer rituals.

What is the difference between a superstition and OCD?

According to *Webster's Eleventh Collegiate Dictionary* (2003), a superstition is "a belief or practice resulting from ignorance, fear of the unknown, or trust in magic or chance." Upon considering this definition, it is possible to see how a superstition and an obsession could be related to each other. Obsessions are often the result of the fear of the unknown, or a belief that things happen to you by chance more than they do to other people. However, just because you have a superstition does not mean that you have OCD. In order to meet the diagnosis of OCD, a person must attempt to ignore or suppress the obsession or somehow neutralize it. Usually people with superstitions do not try to hide them; in fact, they are typically very vocal about them. As a result of a superstition, a person may perform a ritual as a way to undo the effect of the superstition (such as saying "bless you" after a person sneezes in order to prevent their soul, which could be ejected from the body by a sneeze, from being taken by the devil). However, this behavior does not meet the criteria for OCD because the ritual could be performed in many different ways—people vary their exact words, saying "bless you," " "blessings," "god bless you," and so on—and people often say the words quickly, almost without thinking and with very little fanfare. A ritual is the exact opposite—it is typically exact and it often, but not always, involves several steps and can be quite prolonged.

It is possible that superstitious behavior could lead to OCD, but just because someone is superstitious does not mean that that person has, or will develop, OCD.

Chapter 5

COMPULSIONS

- Do people with OCD really spend hours a day straightening fringe on rugs and curtains?
- My hands are cracked and peeling from so much washing, yet I cannot stop myself from doing it—why can't I stop even when it hurts?
- If someone touches me on my left side, I purposely have something touch my right side to be "even." Why is that?
- My husband is very bright, but he is in danger of losing his job because he is so far behind at work. He says that he is too afraid to turn in anything to his boss that is not perfect, so he goes over and over things constantly. Could this be related to OCD?
- My niece calls me every day to get reassurance that she does not have HIV. I always tell her that she is fine and does not need to worry about it. Is this the right thing to do?
- My daughter cannot leave anything until it is completely finished—to the point that she will miss cheerleading practice in order to hang up her clothes. Is this OCD?
- My son is very smart, but he has started failing all of his classes. He can do the work, but he refuses to, saying that he is too afraid of not getting a good grade. Could this be OCD?
- If I check something several times, does that mean that I suffer from OCD?
- I try on ten to fifteen different outfits every morning, and sometimes it even makes me late for work. Could this be an OCD behavior?
- My OCD really annoys me, so why is it so hard to stop doing the rituals?
- The more that others get annoyed with my rituals, the more I seem to need to ritualize—why is that?
- Why do people hoard so many things in their homes, even when it is a danger to themselves or their families?
- Are compulsions always physical, or can people perform mental compulsions?
- If I fix one compulsion, will another one just take its place?
- Am I the only one who does_____?
- A therapist told me that doing a ritual was a "safety-seeking behavior." What does that mean?
- Some of these things sound absolutely ridiculous. How do therapists keep a straight face when they hear about some of these obsessions or compulsions?

Do people with OCD really spend hours a day straightening fringe on rugs and curtains?

Not all people with OCD do this, but some surely do. They are look-ing for symmetry, and they have the idea that if things are not all the same or do not all look the same, something bad will happen, or they won't be able to handle it. In order to avoid this, they may vacuum in only one direction, make sure that their feet leave identical look-ing footprints on the carpet, or actually get on the floor and comb the fibers on the carpet until they are all even and going in the same direction. This can obviously take hours each day.

A documentary made about OCD in 2002, OCD: *The War Inside*, featured a boy who felt he had to leave all of the carpet fibers on the stairs facing the same direction, so he performed an elaborate ritual to walk up the stairs. If he made a mistake on any stair, he would have to go all the way back down to the first stair and start over again. He said that there were days that it would take him hours to walk upstairs to his room.

Why not just take the carpet off the stairs, you might ask? Although this may seem to be a quick fix, it does not address the fundamental issue—he needed therapy to learn how to face this sort of problem. Just because he may not have carpet in his home does not mean that he will never encounter carpeting again or that the pattern of obsessive thoughts and compulsive behaviors won't man-ifest itself in another way. Therefore, his best option was to leave the carpeting there and learn how to handle it and fight the disorder, which is what happened.

My hands are cracked and peeling from so much washing, yet I cannot stop myself from doing it— why can't I stop even when it hurts?

The relief that you get from washing your hands outweighs any pain or injury that you experience when your hands become raw from the constant scouring. Think of the scales of justice—a scale with two plates hanging off either side of a bar, which is balancing on a point in the center of the bar. Place a weight on one side, and that side goes down, while the other side rises. Using this image, think about relief from obsessive thoughts on one plate and pain caused by the rituals on the other plate. As long as the relief of the ritual outweighs the pain that it causes, you will continue to do it. Only by facing your fear of not doing the ritual and realizing that the feared consequence will not occur will you begin to shift the weights on the scale and start to recognize that the damage you are causing to your hands is actually more dangerous than not performing the ritual.

If someone touches me on my left side, I purposely have something touch my right side to be "even." Why is that?

This is a form of OCD referred to as symmetry. When people with OCD have symmetry concerns, they want things to be even or balanced. Therefore, they may do things an even numbers of times— they may walk in and out of doors twice to enter a room with both their left and then right feet first, or they may want to be sure that if one side of their body was touched, the other side gets the same touch. Some individuals with symmetry OCD have gone to the point of injuring the non-injured side of their bodies so that they could have symmetrical pains or scars.

Symmetry compulsions can be driven by obsessions (if I do not do this in balance, my life will be out of balance), or it can just be a compulsive behavior that people develop, something that just feels as if it is the right way to do things.

My husband is very bright, but he is in danger of losing his job because he is so far behind at work. He says that he is too afraid to turn in anything to his boss that is not perfect, so he goes over and over things constantly. Could this be related to OCD?

This may very well be related to OCD. Many times, individuals with OCD fear not being perfect, so they look over things repeatedly, do far more research than is necessary, or do not turn things in because they are afraid of the consequences of not being perfect. Your husband may believe that turning in something that is less than perfect is worse than not turning it in at all, possibly hoping his boss will just forget about the task. However, as this behavior continues, your husband will become more and more fearful of not being perfect as he gets increasing pressure from his boss to actually complete his duties. Your husband could very possibly lose his job over this, and it is important for him to get some help so that he can start to be productive at work. Many companies have an employee assistance program (EAP) that he can contact for free and that can help him find a therapist who could aid him in fixing this problem. (There will be more on this in Chapter 9.)

My niece calls me every day to get reassurance that she does not have HIV. I always tell her that she is fine and does not need to worry about it. Is this the right thing to do?

Although you may feel as if telling her she is fine is the right thing to do, it will most likely lead her to feel worse in the long run. There are several reasons for this.

There are two types of reward systems at work here: short-term rewards and long-term rewards. Each time your niece calls you, she is seeking to feel better right away—this is a short-term reward. Think about a grocery store. They put that candy right at the check-out aisle, and you and your child have to stand next to it, look at it, and smell it. If your child asks for candy, and you say, "No," your child may start to scream and cry and throw a tantrum. If you tell her that she can have the candy if she just stops crying, you have just taught her a way to guarantee getting candy (short-term reward)—throwing a tantrum. The chances of her having a tantrum the next time you are near the candy have now increased. Or, you could have let her cry and scream while you checked out, and then left the store, teaching her that throwing a tantrum will get her nowhere and therefore decreasing the chance of a tantrum in the future.

Similarly, your niece received a short-term reward from you when you told her that she will be fine. She will now be more likely to want that reward again because it relieved her anxiety so quickly. This makes sense—why wouldn't people want quick relief? Yet this is also the problem. Because that quick relief feels so good, she will not face her anxiety and learn to handle it in the long term. Also, every time you tell her that she is fine, she feels that she is no longer responsible for anything bad happening—you are. Because you gave her reassurance about her health, you are the one who is now responsible for her health—if something bad does happen to her, she is going to blame you for it, thinking you lied to her.

What will most likely happen is she will call more and more, maybe up to one hundred times a day. Therefore, as difficult as it may be, you need to start to decrease your role in her OCD. You can cut your reassurance-giving down to every other call, and then every third call, and so on, until you finally tell her that you are no longer going to answer her questions because your reassurance is helping her to actually maintain her OCD instead of decreasing its effects on her life. If she protests, it may be a good time to suggest some professional help.

And, of course, if she is involved in at-risk behavior that could lead to HIV, she should be tested and seek help immediately. However, most people with OCD are not involved in these behaviors, yet they still fear the chance of getting the disease.

My daughter cannot leave anything until it is completely finished—to the point that she will miss cheerleading practice in order to hang up her clothes. Is this OCD?

This may very well meet the criteria for OCD. It is important to first see why she is doing these things, even at the expense of missing practice. If it's because she is afraid that she will be punished for not completing her chores before she leaves the home, then this is not OCD. If she is doing this as a way to avoid cheerleading and to get kicked off of the team, this also is not OCD. Both of these scenarios may be possible, so it is important to truly look at all possibilities before diagnosing someone with OCD.

However, if she is doing this because she fears that she will not be able to concentrate and will only be able to think of her clothes being out of order, which will mess up her cheers, she may be spending the extra time to put her clothes away to try to help her cheerleading—even at the expense of not being able to get to practice with the team. She may see it as better to be late and do well than to be on time and distracted, which is a fairly sure sign of OCD.

My son is very smart, but he has started failing all of his classes. He can do the work, but he refuses to, saying that he is too afraid of not getting a good grade. Could this be OCD?

Absolutely. There are many children who are excellent students who do not do their work for the simple reason that they fear getting anything but an A. They may see a B as a failure or may fear that others will not think they are smart if they do not get an A. Therefore, to avoid this, they may not do any of their work and may wind up receiving all Fs. Even though they get failing grades, they may take comfort in the fact that the grades are due to their not doing the work instead of a reflection of the fact that someone did not think the work that they did was of enough quality to receive an A. If this is the reason your son is failing, you should consider taking him to a therapist.

If I check something several times, does that mean that I suffer from OCD?

No, it does not. Many of us double- and triple-check things. Take a man who pre-measures any construction work he does three times (just for projects around the house—he is not a carpenter). He does this to be sure that he has exactly the right measurements so that everything lines up when he begins the assembly process. This is just a part of his routine. It does not interfere with his life, cause him undue stress, or take more than an hour out of his average day.

Without any level of stress or interference, this is just a routine and not a ritual that is done to neutralize an obsession. And the project still gets done, even though the extra measuring may add an additional twenty minutes to the total completion time. If an OCD ritual were involved, there would be a thought associated with the measurement, such as, "I have to get this perfect, or I will never be able to enjoy the finished product because I will know it has a flaw." Or the person could have an image of the finished product collapsing because of a measurement being off by one-sixteenth of an inch. Because of these thoughts or images, a person with OCD might measure a board fifty times, put it up, and then take it back down and do this again and again because it just did not look right or seem to fit perfectly. Or he might hire others to do the project, only to stand over them the entire time they are working, telling them to redo things or make changes.

We all have things that we check maybe a little more than is necessary in order to make ourselves comfortable. It is when these things start to interfere with our lives that it starts being a disorder. Therefore, if the checking does not interfere with your life, or you would feel fine if one day you were not able to check the object of your focus, then this behavior would not meet the criteria for OCD.

I try on ten to fifteen different outfits every morning, and sometimes it even makes me late for work. Could this be an OCD behavior?

It could be several things. It could be OCD if you keep putting things on until something just "feels right." Remember that we discussed how OCD often searches for something to feel right, even though what feels right can change on a daily, even hourly, basis. Or, some people put certain fears onto clothes, thinking that wearing certain outfits may cause them to be bad people or to somehow change their sexual preferences.

This could also be a symptom of a social anxiety disorder, if, for example, you look at an outfit and then think of all of the negative things that people may say or think about you if you were to wear that outfit, so you change again and again until you put on something that you finally think will not lead you to be judged negatively that day. If the clothes-changing is to the point that it is negatively affecting your life, you may want to speak to a therapist about it.

My OCD really annoys me, so why is it so hard to stop doing the rituals?

When you perform compulsive behaviors, you feel either a relief from the obsessions or as if you have somehow averted an unwanted consequence. As long as that relief is strong, you will want to continue doing the rituals, and until your level of annoyance with the rituals is actually greater than the level of relief you get from performing them, you'll keep doing them.

Although most people with OCD are able to recognize *after* performing a ritual that they really did not need to do it, it is at the time that the ritual is being performed that they need to intervene and face their anxiety in the situation. If they do this and allow themselves to see that they can actually handle it and that nothing bad will come of it, then they will be less likely to do the ritual again in the future.

The more that others get annoyed with my rituals, the more I seem to need to ritualize—why is that?

This is probably a result of your frustration with yourself. As you perceive others getting annoyed with you, you get frustrated and your anxiety increases. When this occurs, it becomes harder to concentrate and focus on the task at hand, and that distraction makes it more difficult to perform your rituals correctly.

This is especially true for individuals who are perfectionists. If you fear that people will judge you if you do not do things perfectly, you may interpret people's annoyance at your rituals as actually being annoyance at your not doing things perfectly. This can unfortunately reinforce the idea that people would accept you more if you did everything perfectly. As you put more pressure on yourself to conform to these expectations, then you will have a harder time actually satisfying them, and the cycle will just get worse and worse.

Why do people hoard so many things in their homes, even when it is a danger to themselves or their families?

Individuals may hoard things for several reasons. Some people have trouble passing up a bargain, and even though they may already have several meat thermometers, for example, seeing one on sale for only 99 cents becomes too much of a temptation to pass up. Another example would be someone driving by a house on garbage day and picking up an old lawn mower sitting by the curb. She may think she could fix it or take it to a scrap metal recycler. Hoarders who like the idea of fixing machines would find it almost impossible to not pick up the mower, even though they may already have seven mowers that need fixing at their home already. Or perhaps hoarders may be unable to get rid of things because of sentimental value, fearing that throwing out an item would lead to the loss of all of the memories associated with that item (such as forgetting about a baseball game you attended if you were to discard a souvenir mug from the game, even though it is cracked, and even though you have twelve other identical mugs from the other games that you went to that season). Hoarding can become a danger to people for several reasons. A person's house may be so cluttered that it is easy to trip over things and fall. Further, the cluttered items can be a fire hazard. Or all of the items may be so tightly packed that they may actually block off essential parts of a home, such as access to a furnace or circuit breaker.

People hoard all of these items because the fear of discarding them is greater than their fear of the danger the items actually create.

Unfortunately, hoarders may even choose their possessions over their own hygiene or over family members (some family members choose to move out of the home rather than live with all of the items cluttering the home). However, there is hope for treating hoarders, and several new assessment tools and therapies are being researched to assist hoarders and their families. The OCF website (www.ocfoundation.org) also has an excellent section on hoarding.

Are compulsions always physical, or can people perform mental compulsions?

People can definitely perform mental compulsions. Some examples of mental compulsions would be saying prayers over and over again until they are said "just right," repeating the name of someone you thought something negative about to try to undo the "bad" thought, or counting up to certain lucky numbers to prevent a feared consequence. All of these compulsions can be performed without anyone actually noticing them being performed. However, as the compulsions increase over time, the individual performing them becomes more and more preoccupied with doing the mental compulsions, and they appear distracted more and more often. Eventually, individuals with mental compulsions can spend hours in their head, fearing their thoughts and attempting to undo the effects of those thoughts with other thoughts. However, therapy is effective for mental compulsions as well as physical compulsions, with the focus of the therapy being acceptance of the thoughts and decreasing the attempts to mentally undo the thoughts.

For example, some people compulsively count things, such as ceiling tiles, carpet squares, or the number of steps that they take. One way to start challenging this is to have them change the way that they count. They can start to count every other step, and then every third step, and so on until they are barely counting at all—eventually, they'll stop altogether. Just changing your rituals can have a major impact on your giving them up because you allow yourself to see that there really is not a correct way to do them, and if there is no correct way to do them, then maybe they do not even have to be done.

If I fix one compulsion, will another one just take its place?

The idea that something else will replace a compulsion you have overcome is called symptom substitution, and it was an early critique of cognitive behavioral therapy (CBT) and exposure and response prevention (ERP). Because of the adherence of old-school psychologists and psychiatrists to Freud's psychoanalysis, many doctors clung to the idea that talk therapy, and not behavioral therapy, was the only real way to solve a mental problem. They believed that some type of inner pain or conflict must set off OCD. Because CBT and ERP therapists did not "work through" that inner pain, the idea was that once the patient worked on adjusting his behavior to eliminate one ritual, another would just take its place as the new way that inner pain would rear its ugly head.

But research has shown that this is not the case, and it is not true that if you work through a compulsion, another one will automatically take its place. It is possible that there will be other compulsions, but that is largely because most people with OCD suffer from more than one compulsion. Any other ritual that appears was probably just not as apparent as the one that was eliminated through therapy. So if you deal with one ritual, you move on to the next one until they have all been addressed in therapy.

Am I the only one that does_____?

Probably not. Many patients enter therapists' offices ashamed of their behaviors. They are reluctant to talk about their OCD obsessions or compulsions, but when they eventually share their concerns with their doctor or therapist, they are often shocked to hear that the therapist has worked with many individuals who have had the same or similar thoughts or compulsions.

It is unfortunate that the shame many people feel about their obsessions or compulsions is often what delays their getting help— just hoping that the intrusive thoughts and actions will go away on their own can lead to them becoming much worse. What people with OCD need to realize is that they are not bad people for having obsessions, just like someone with cancer is not a bad person for having a tumor. But in our society, we think that it is acceptable to be out of control of some of our bodily processes, such as a tumor, whereas we must always be in total control of our mind. As long as this unfortunate belief remains, then we will continue to perpetrate the negative stigma of mental illness. OCD is a treatable disorder, and there should be no shame in seeking help.

A therapist told me that doing a ritual was a "safety-seeking behavior." What does that mean?

You are performing the ritual to try to feel safe because you fear the obsessive thought, impulse, or image. This safety-seeking behavior is what will maintain your OCD because after a while, you will feel as if the only way to be safe is to perform the ritual. Then you will feel stuck, because now not performing the ritual would be unsafe, and no one wants to put him- or herself in an unsafe position.

In order to see improvement, you have to start to decrease your safety-seeking behavior and start to expose yourself to the things that you fear without doing rituals. Once you do this and recognize that the feared consequences will not occur, you will probably see a decrease in your OCD.

Some of these things sound absolutely ridiculous. How do therapists keep a straight face when they hear about some of these obsessions or compulsions?

Those of us who specialize in OCD treatment hear these stories every day, and after a while, not much surprises us. In fact, patients are often reluctant to tell us some of their "worst" obsessive thoughts for fear that we will think they are crazy or that we might laugh at them. When we tell them that we have heard the same thing from many other patients, they are often stunned. But, it's the truth.

However, the main reason that we do not laugh at our patients is that we can understand how difficult it is for them to live with this disorder. OCD can be devastating. To constantly fear that you will harm or have harmed people, to think that you are contaminated, or to have a nagging thought in the back of your head that you did something wrong that will just not go away—these are all very serious concerns. Those of us who work with OCD patients understand how this can affect a person's entire life, and we understand that they want, more than anything, to be free of their OCD. Yet challenging their OCD is what they fear most—because they so fervently believe that if they do not do the rituals, bad things will happen.

Over time, as a person sees improvement, a therapist and his or her patient can look back at some things and chuckle together about what behaviors the person used to do, but a therapist would never behave this way when first meeting a patient or as a way to tease a patient. If your therapist does something like this that in any way makes you uncomfortable, think about confronting the therapist to let him or her know that your feelings have been hurt, or consider finding a new therapist as soon as possible.

Chapter 6

OCD AND ITS RELATIONSHIP WITH OTHER DISORDERS

- What is a mental disorder?
- Is OCD the same thing as an anxiety disorder?
- What are the anxiety disorders?
- What is the difference between a phobia and OCD?
- What is the difference between posttraumatic stress disorder and OCD?
- What is the difference between generalized anxiety disorder and OCD?
- What is the difference between agoraphobia and OCD?
- I am embarrassed to go out in public because of some of my rituals. Does that mean I have social phobia?
- Sometimes I have a panic attack when I cannot do my rituals "just right." Does this mean I have panic disorder in addition to OCD?
- What is an OCD spectrum disorder?
- How are OCD and Tourette's disorder related?
- How are OCD and trichotillomania related?
- How are OCD and skin picking related?
- How are OCD and body dysmorphic disorder (BDD) related?
- How are OCD and kleptomania related to each other?
- How are OCD and pyromania related to each other?
- How are OCD and delusional disorder related?
- How are OCD and hypochondriasis related to each other?
- What is the difference between an eating disorder and OCD?
- My daughter has an eating disorder, and she has a lot of rituals surrounding her eating. Could she also have OCD?
- Are cutting (self-mutilation) and OCD related?
- How is OCD related to attention deficit-hyperactivity disorder (ADHD)?
- Is there a link between OCD and autism?

- Is there a link between OCD and Asperger's disorder?
- Is major depressive disorder common in people with OCD?
- Is worrying a part of OCD?
- How can coexisting conditions complicate OCD (or vice versa)?
- How can stress levels affect OCD?
- What is obsessive-compulsive personality disorder?
- What is the difference between OCD and OCPD?

What is a mental disorder?

Unfortunately, there is really no agreed-upon definition of what a mental disorder is. Here is the outline that the developers of the *DSM-IV-TR* (2000) used as their guide (as we learn more about mental disorders, these criteria are subject to change):

A clinically significant behavioral or psychological syndrome or pattern that occurs in an individual and that is associated with present distress, disability, or a significantly increased risk for suffering.

A mental disorder is basically a way of thinking, behaving, or acting that causes distress in a person's life. This does not include grief over the loss of a loved one or hardships beyond an individual's control (such as a flood), unless the reaction of the person goes beyond what would normally be expected for someone in the same situation.

Although the overall definition of a mental disorder may be difficult to pin down, there are definitive ways to classify individual disorders, as discussed in subsequent questions and answers.

Is OCD the same thing as an anxiety disorder?

OCD is an anxiety disorder, and there are several anxiety disorders which we will discuss in the following pages. First, the basis of anxiety disorders is fear, and fear can be experienced in many ways. The most basic fear experience is a panic attack. A panic attack is an intense feeling of fear that reaches a peak within ten minutes and has four or more of the following symptoms:

- pounding heart
- sweating
- trembling or shaking
- shortness of breath
- choking feelings
- chest pain or discomfort
- nausea or abdominal distress
- feelings of dizziness, unsteadiness, light-headedness, or faintness
- derealization (feeling out of touch with reality) or depersonalization (feeling outside of one's body)
- fear of losing control or going crazy
- fear of dying
- numbness or tingling sensations
- chills or hot flashes

Panic attacks can occur in relation to specific fears, such as prior to giving a speech, or they can occur at random times throughout the day. Panic attacks can also occur in relation to OCD because people may get so stressed about their obsessions or compulsions that the stress may lead them to having a panic attack. Or if they are unable to complete their compulsion, that may also trigger a panic attack.

What are the anxiety disorders?

The following list describes all of the diagnosable anxiety disorders:

- **Panic disorder with or without agoraphobia:** The occurrence of panic attacks out of the blue, along with fears of future attacks, worry about the consequences of the attack (such as a heart attack), or significant behavior changes related to the attacks (such as not working out to avoid your heart rate going above a certain number). Panic disorder is diagnosed either with or without agoraphobia (see next paragraph).

- **Agoraphobia without history of panic disorder:** A fear of places or situations in which escape may be difficult or help might not be available if a panic attack or panic symptoms occur. These situations are generally avoided or endured with significant distress, or a trusted friend or family member is required to go along to ensure that the agoraphobic feels safe. For example, if you once had a panic attack in a movie theater, you may stop going to the movies or only go if someone you trust is with you so that person can help you if you get anxious. Agoraphobia is diagnosed either alone (without history of panic disorder) or in conjunction with panic disorder.

- **Specific phobias:** Specific phobias (such as fears of elevators, planes, heights, and so on) are excessive or unreasonable fears of the presence or the anticipation of an object, situation, or event. Therefore, people with phobias of specific things avoid these things, often at a significant cost to themselves (such as losing their job because of refusing to fly to a business meeting in another city).

- **Obsessive-compulsive disorder:** The presence of obsessive thoughts, impulses, or images and the resulting behaviors (compulsions) performed to undo those thoughts, impulses, or images.

Though it is possible to be diagnosed with OCD while experiencing only obsessions or only compulsions, this is very rare.

- **Social phobia:** The excessive fear of social situations in which a person may be subject to the scrutiny of others or may become embarrassed or humiliated. People with social phobia characteristically exaggerate the consequences that could occur if they were to make a mistake or be judged negatively, so they avoid the situations where this could occur.

- **Posttraumatic stress disorder (PTSD):** The experience of an event that involved the threat of death or serious injury to yourself or someone close to you, or the actual death of that person, and the feelings of fear, helplessness, or horror that result from that event. In response to this event and these feelings, there are experiences of arousal, such as a heightened startle response; experiences of avoidance, such as not going near the place where the event occurred; and the re-experiencing of the event, such as in flashbacks or nightmares. The diagnosis of PTSD is considered when the reaction to the event is still causing significant difficulties four weeks after the trauma occurred.

- **Acute stress disorder:** Similar to posttraumatic stress disorder, but the experience of significant anxiety lasts between two days to four weeks and occurs within four weeks of the traumatic event.

- **Generalized anxiety disorder:** Excessive anxiety and worry over the course of six months or more about several different topics. Along with the worry, the person experiences symptoms such as difficulty concentrating, fatigue, irritability, restlessness, muscle tension, or sleep disturbance. The worry is to such an extent that it causes significant interference in the person's life.

- **Anxiety disorder not otherwise specified:** When a person is experiencing significant anxiety symptoms, but they do not fall neatly into any of the categories above, the diagnosis of anxiety disorder not otherwise specified can be given.

All of the anxiety disorders are based in the fear center of the brain, and with all of them there is an overactive fear response to some type of cue or stressor, which causes significant interference in the person's life.

What is the difference between a phobia and OCD?

A phobia is a fear of a specific object, event, or situation and the resulting attempts to avoid the feared thing. This can sound similar to OCD, and people often confuse the two disorders. Many people will say that they are afraid of flying. If people can get on a plane after doing some rituals that they feel will make them safe and that will counter the obsessions that they have about flying (an image of the plane falling from the sky), then they may have OCD. However, if they have a flying phobia, there is not much that they can do to make the fear go away (without some therapy or self-help assistance), and they avoid flying at all costs—even if it means losing their job—then that is a specific phobia. Specific phobias are typically limited to one thing, whereas OCD is usually more general. Individuals with a flying phobia may have no problems with any other type of travel, whereas people whose OCD is focused on travel will have obsessions and compulsions about any mode of transport.

What is the difference between posttraumatic stress disorder and OCD?

While there do appear to be some similarities between OCD and posttraumatic stress disorder (PTSD), there are also several differences. First, PTSD has a defined trigger, a traumatic event that kicks it off, while OCD need not have a specific trigger that sets it off. Also, while PTSD does involve unwanted thoughts, often in the form of flashbacks or nightmares about the trauma, it is limited to the theme of the trauma. OCD thoughts can run the gamut of themes and need not be related to anything traumatic that has actually happened. In fact, OCD thoughts are often about traumas that *might* happen instead of ones that have happened. Further, there are avoidance behaviors often associated with PTSD, such as avoiding the place where a trauma occurred, but there are no compulsive behaviors that are associated with PTSD, as there are in OCD.

What is the difference between generalized anxiety disorder and OCD?

The worries in generalized anxiety disorder (GAD) are typically worries about real life problems, while OCD worries are often beyond what would be expected in real life, or to such a small probability that it really makes no logical sense to actually spend time thinking about it. Also, in OCD, the thoughts can often take the form of impulses or images, while in GAD, the thoughts are typically just thoughts (e.g., what if I lose my job, what if my car breaks down, what if I don't do well in school, etc.). Further, there are no compulsions done in GAD to get rid of the thoughts, while people with OCD do perform compulsive behaviors to somehow neutralize their thoughts. Finally, there are several physical or mental symptoms associated with GAD (e.g. restlessness, irritability, muscle tension, etc.) that need not be present for the diagnosis of OCD.

What is the difference between agoraphobia and OCD?

While individuals with agoraphobia avoid certain things, as someone with OCD may also do, the reason for the avoidance in agoraphobia is to avoid the occurrence of a panic attack or panic symptoms, while the avoidance in OCD may be due to numerous reasons, such as fears of contamination or to avoid having to do a ritual. Therefore, the avoidance in OCD is much broader than the very specific avoidance of panic symptoms found in agoraphobia.

I am embarrassed to go out in public because of some of my rituals. Does that mean I have social phobia?

Although one of the criteria for social phobia is that sufferers avoid places or situations where they may become embarrassed, avoiding places over the specific embarrassment of doing rituals in public would not meet the definition of social phobia. The *DSM-IV-TR* (2000) requires that the symptoms of a disorder not be better accounted for by another diagnosis. If the embarrassment were not because of the rituals, but because of a fear of being humiliated in public, then it would more likely be social phobia. If the embarrassment is over a ritual, OCD better accounts for the embarrassment because if you did not have OCD, then you would not be performing rituals that are embarrassing.

Sometimes I have a panic attack when I cannot do my rituals "just right." Does this mean I have panic disorder in addition to OCD?

Just because you have a panic attack does not mean that you have panic disorder. Panic attacks can occur when you are very anxious, scared, or frightened. Not being able to perform a ritual "just right" can evoke a great deal of anxiety for a person with OCD, and it is possible that a panic attack could be the result of that anxiety.

For a diagnosis of panic disorder, panic attacks need to occur out of the blue. Because the panic attacks mentioned here are related to the inability to complete a ritual, they are related to an event and not just randomly occurring. Therefore, panic attacks in this instance are a result of the OCD and the difficulty with completing the ritual, and not a result of panic disorder.

What is an OCD spectrum disorder?

An OCD spectrum disorder is a disorder that is different from, but appears to be related to, OCD. Several possible factors point to a relationship between these disorders:

1. The psychological treatments that work for OCD also work for these disorders.
2. The medications that work for OCD also work for these disorders.
3. These disorders have a high comorbidity (co-occurrence) with OCD.
4. Areas in the brain that are affected by OCD are affected by these other disorders.
5. There appears to be a family history of these disorders as well as OCD in many families.

Disorders that are considered to be in the spectrum of OCD are as follows:

1. tic disorders
2. eating disorders
3. impulse-control disorders
4. somatoform disorders

All of these disorders are addressed in later questions.

How are OCD and Tourette's disorder related?

There is a probable biological relationship between OCD and Tourette's disorder because individuals with Tourette's disorder are more likely to have OCD than are individuals with most other mental health disorders. Tourette's is a tic disorder, and tics, according to the *DSM-IV-TR* (2000), are "sudden, rapid, recurrent, non-rhythmic, stereotyped motor movements or vocalizations." The tics are classified as either simple or complex, depending on the amount of time it takes to complete the tic or how involved the tic is (such as an eye blink versus an entire bodily movement).

To differentiate Tourette's and OCD, we need to look at the defining characteristics of the two disorders. For OCD, the ritual must be done as a response to an obsession or according to strict rules. A tic, on the other hand, is performed to relieve some type of physical tension that is occurring. If there is an obsession, it's OCD. If there is no obsession, but the behavior is still very purposeful and follows very set rules, then OCD is also warranted. If the behavior is performed out of the blue for no purpose other than to relieve tension, then it is probably a tic and is probably part of Tourette's or one of the other tic disorders (chronic motor or vocal tic disorder, transient tic disorder, or tic disorder not otherwise specified).

If both criteria are met, a diagnosis of both OCD and Tourette's disorder is possible. The criteria for Tourette's disorder, according to the *DSM-IV-TR* (2000), are as follows:

1. Multiple motor tics and one or more vocal tics
2. The tics occur many times a day or nearly every day over the course of a year, with no more than a three-month tic-free period.
3. The onset is before the age of 18.

4. The Tourette's is not better accounted for by the effects of a substance or a medical condition.

So, an individual may have motor and vocal tics that they perform in addition to the occurrence of obsessions or compulsions. If this were to happen, then the diagnosis of both disorders would be in order.

How are OCD and trichotillomania related?

According to the *DSM-IV-TR* (2000), trichotillomania, or TTM, is the repeated pulling out of one's hair (from any part of the body). It is associated with tension prior to pulling out the hair, or when trying to resist pulling the hair, and a feeling of relief when the hair is pulled out. Sometimes the hair is discarded, and other times it is eaten, which can lead to serious medical complications because hair is not easily digested and can form into an intestinal blockage over time.

Although it is not uncommon to find people who have both OCD and TTM (15 to 30 percent of individuals with one of the diagnoses will have the other as well), there are differences between the two disorders. Individuals with TTM do not pull the hair out in response to an obsessive thought. If that is the reason for the hair pulling, the diagnosis is OCD. Also, there is not typically a set pattern or way to pull the hair out in TTM. It is the removal of the hair that is most important—not how it is removed. If it were OCD, there would be a ritual for it.

Trichotillomania does appear similar to OCD, and, in fact, it is more related to OCD than it is to any of the other anxiety disorders. Exactly how the two are related to each other is being researched, but it appears that people with disorders that involve repeated behaviors, such as TTM, OCD, and skin picking, have shown similarities in brain structure and imaging. There are also certain areas in the brain that show similar activity levels in patients with OCD and TTM. Further, TTM and OCD both show responses to cognitive behavioral therapy (CBT), and their response to medications that treat obsessions also appear to be similar in some studies, but vastly different in others. This just shows how young we are in our ability to understand, on a chemical or brain-structure level, just how the brain functions.

Further research needs to be done to see just how related TTM and OCD are, but it does appear from the current research that they may be more alike than different.

How are OCD and skin picking related?

Skin picking is, according to the *DSM-IV-TR* (2000), an impulse-control disorder not otherwise specified (NOS), which means it meets the criteria for an impulse-control disorder, but there are not specific diagnostic criteria for skin picking.

Impulse-control disorders are defined as disorders in which individuals have difficulty in resisting the performance of an impulse or drive that is harmful to themselves or someone else. Typically, there is a sense of tension prior to performing the act and then a sense of relief or pleasure after the act is completed. Some impulse-control disorders are kleptomania (stealing objects that are not actually needed), pyromania (fire setting), or trichotillomania, as discussed previously.

In skin picking, individuals pick at their skin, causing damage to it, as a way to relieve tension and experience relief from that tension. One possible reason for this behavior is that it is distracting, in the sense that it is easier to focus on the skin picking than some other stressors in life. Also, some people feel that skin picking is under their control, versus external stressors that are not, and they would rather be involved in a behavior that they can control versus something that they cannot.

For individuals who do meet the criteria for impulse-control disorder NOS with a focus on skin picking, there is a 22 percent chance that they will also have OCD, according to the most recent research.

How are OCD and body dysmorphic disorder (BDD) related?

Body dysmorphic disorder (BDD) is, according to the *DSM-IV-TR* (2000), a somatoform disorder: It has physical symptoms that suggest the presence of a general medical condition, but cannot be fully explained by a medical condition. In BDD, the person is overwhelmingly, almost obsessively, concerned about an imagined or slight physical defect. This preoccupation causes interference in the person's daily functioning.

Individuals with BDD may avoid leaving their home without spending several hours applying makeup to cover up a blemish that may or may not be visible to others, they may go out only with a hat on if they fear that their hair is thinning, or they may seek out expensive surgical procedures to correct any slight anomalies they think keep them from looking perfect.

Individuals with BDD often seek reassurance that they look decent, but often do not believe anyone who tells them that they do (they often respond by saying that people just tell them they look OK because they are being nice). However, if someone were to tell them that they did not look acceptable, they would believe that and use it as further evidence that they were correct in their beliefs.

Individuals with BDD may have obsessions about their looks and even perform compulsive behaviors, such as constantly looking in the mirror, but they would be diagnosed with OCD only if there were other obsessions or compulsions present that did not focus on their BDD concerns. Research indicates that between 16 and 37 percent of individuals with BDD have OCD, and vice versa. Further, the treatments for OCD appear to also work well for BDD. There is a great deal of information available about BDD, and several organizations are devoted to its research and treatment, many of which can be found at BDD Central (http://www.bddcentral.com/mainpage.htm).

How are OCD and kleptomania related to each other?

According to the *DSM-IV-TR* (2000), kleptomania is the "recurrent failure to resist the impulses to steal objects that are not needed for personal use or for their monetary value." Prior to the stealing, there is an increase of tension, and after the theft, that tension is relieved. Further, "the stealing is not committed to express anger or vengeance," nor is it better accounted for by another disorder, such as antisocial personality disorder, or in response to a hallucination.

Although OCD involves compulsive behaviors that neutralize obsessive impulses, if those impulses and behaviors are strictly limited to stealing, then Kleptomania better accounts for the problem than OCD. If there are impulses beyond stealing, then it's likely OCD.

Research also indicates that the relatives of individuals with kleptomania have higher rates of OCD than are found in the general population.

How are OCD and pyromania related to each other?

Pyromania is, according to the *DSM-IV-TR* (2000), "deliberate and purposeful fire setting on more than one occasion." Prior to the act of fire setting, there is an increase in tension, and there is a long-held fascination with fire. Once the fire is set, there is a sense of relief or joy. Fires set by people with pyromania are not set for vengeance or for monetary gain and are not better accounted for by another disorder, such as delusional disorder or antisocial personality disorder.

Similar to the other disorders that we have discussed, pyromania and OCD can appear similar on the surface. The main difference between the two is that if the obsession and compulsion are limited to fire setting, the diagnosis is pyromania, but if there are other obsessive impulses or compulsive behaviors, then OCD would be the appropriate diagnosis.

How are OCD and delusional disorder related?

Delusional disorder is defined by the *DSM-IV-TR* (2000) as a month or more of nonbizarre delusions. A delusion is a "false belief based on incorrect inference about external reality that is sustained despite what almost everyone else believes and despite what constitutes incontrovertible and obvious proof or evidence to the contrary." Or, to put it in laymen's terms, a delusion is a belief that a person holds onto very strongly despite the fact that no one else believes it or that there is overwhelming evidence to the contrary, or both.

Bizarre delusions are those that are almost, if not completely, impossible in reality, such as aliens replacing your brain with a machine that they use to download information, whereas nonbizarre delusions could be things that could actually happen, but are unlikely, such as being loved by a model you've never met or being slowly poisoned by your neighbor.

Individuals with delusional disorder do not necessarily suffer from schizophrenia, they may show no other impairment in functioning, they are not suffering from a long standing mood disorder (such as major depressive disorder or bipolar disorder), and they are not experiencing their nonbizarre delusions because of substance abuse or a medical condition.

The best way to differentiate between OCD and delusional disorder is that a person with OCD recognizes that their obsessions or compulsions are excessive, whereas someone with delusional disorder would not know that their beliefs are not realistic. However, there are individuals with OCD who are less able than others to recognize the excessiveness of some of their beliefs or behaviors, and therefore the diagnosis of both disorders at the same time is possible. In this case, what would typically happen in therapy is that a person would be prescribed an atypical antipsychotic medication to decrease the strength of the obsessions, and then some CBT and ERP would be tried to deal with the compulsions.

How are OCD and hypochondriasis related to each other?

According to the *DSM-IV-TR* (2000), hypochondriasis is the "preoccupation of having, or the idea that one has, a serious disease based on the person's misinterpretation of bodily sensations." In addition to this, the person believes that he or she is ill despite the results of medical testing, and that belief leads to impairment in social, occupational, or other types of functioning. Further, for diagnosis of hypochondriasis, the person must not have a delusional disorder, and the person's belief that he or she is ill must be ongoing for at least 6 months.

OCD is different from hypochondriasis in that, even if one of the foci of the OCD is medical concerns, individuals will also have other obsessions and unrelated compulsions, such as compulsively straightening things. If the focus is only on illness or disease, then hypochondriasis is the appropriate diagnosis.

What is the difference between an eating disorder and OCD?

According to the *DSM-IV-TR* (2000), eating disorders are "character-ized by severe disturbances in eating behavior." The disturbances manifest themselves in over- or underfeeding or the repeated binge eating of food followed by purging with vomiting, laxatives, exces-sive exercise, and so on.

Eating disorders are often marked by an obsession with food, with sufferers constantly thinking about it and using it as a way to create control and perfection. The typical mindset behind an eating disor-der is that the only thing that people can really be in control of is the amount of food they take in, so if being thin is perfect, then they can become perfect by controlling the amount of food that they eat. This sense of control over their weight also leads to a sense of control in their lives. People with anorexia nervosa attempt to gain this control over their weight by eating far less than they should and exercising constantly. Individuals with bulimia nervosa binge on food and then purge it somehow to regain control over the food. Needless to say, both of these disorders are very dangerous, and eating disorders have the highest mortality rate of any mental health disorder.

Research indicates that anywhere from 18 to 37 percent of indi-viduals with an eating disorder also have OCD. Also, recent research has indicated that females who develop OCD prior to adolescence have around a 40 percent chance of developing an eating disorder in adolescence. Therefore, it appears that there is a rather strong rela-tionship between eating disorders and OCD.

If the obsessions and compulsive behaviors are related only to food, then the diagnosis would be an eating disorder. However, if there are other obsessions and compulsions, the diagnosis of OCD is also warranted.

My daughter has an eating disorder, and she has a lot of rituals surrounding her eating. Could she also have OCD?

Absolutely. As previously discussed, OCD and eating disorders are related to each other. Many individuals with eating disorders also have OCD. In fact, a national treatment center recently opened a combined OCD and eating disorder treatment facility.

Many individuals with eating disorders are attempting to control their bodies. In fact, they often think that the only thing in their life over which they can have total control is the amount of food that they consume or digest. There is also a desire to be seen as perfect, with the notion that the thinner you are, the more perfect you look.

OCD is also related to control and perfectionism—people with OCD often try to control their obsessions by doing a ritual perfectly to rid themselves of the effect of the obsession. Therefore, it is very common to see concurrent eating disorder and OCD symptoms. However, they must be diagnosed separately—OCD and an eating disorder should not be diagnosed according to the same symptom. An obsession or compulsion about food cannot be cited to diagnose both disorders.

For example, a woman may restrict her eating to only celery, mustard, and pickles (all no- or low-calorie foods). Although this may seem to be a compulsion (repeatedly eating only the same things to prevent the feared consequence of gaining weight), an eating disorder, likely anorexia nervosa, is the proper diagnosis because she is attempting to remain thin. However, if she were to also wash her food in a ritualized fashion to prevent herself from being contaminated, then that would constitute a diagnosis of OCD because she would be demonstrating obsessions about germs with the compulsive washing.

Are cutting (self-mutilation) and OCD related?

Individuals who cut have an impulse-control disorder NOS, similar to skin picking. As discussed, impulse-control disorder and OCD are related to each other.

Often when individuals cut, they are attempting one of several things. Some people cut to create pain that will distract them from any other stressors that are going on in their life. Others cut as a way to see that they are still alive—if they bleed, it means that there is something inside of them, even if they feel empty. Finally, some cut as a way to punish themselves for not being perfect, and the scars are a visual reminder of what they will do to themselves for not being perfect.

Individuals may have elaborate cutting rituals, but if cutting is the only ritual, the diagnosis would be impulse-control disorder NOS, and not OCD. However, if there were other ritualistic behaviors involved, then OCD could also be diagnosed.

How is OCD related to attention deficit-hyperactivity disorder (ADHD)?

A relationship between OCD and attention deficit-hyperactivity disorder (ADHD) has been documented, with some research showing that up to 30 percent of people with ADHD also meet the criteria for OCD. The essential difficulties experienced in ADHD, according to the *DSM-IV-TR* (2000), are trouble paying attention, hyperactivity, and impulsivity. Because of the hyperactivity and impulsivity, ADHD results in difficulties with such activities as sitting still, talking excessively, and interrupting others. Individuals with ADHD are also easily distracted, disorganized, and forgetful. Differentiating between ADHD and OCD can be done by considering the source of the inattentive behavior. With OCD, the inattention would be a result of distraction caused by obsessions; for

ADHD, the inattention is in and of itself a hallmark of the disorder. Further, OCD rituals are typically performed to strict standards, whereas hyperactive activity has a "just get it done" feel to it.

Although one disorder does not cause the other disorder, when the two disorders are combined, there can be great difficulties in focusing on everyday life. In addition to the typical distractions experienced because of the ADHD, there is the added distraction of the obsessive thoughts. Added to the impulsivity of the ADHD, the rituals can also appear impulsive.

Individuals diagnosed with both disorders would benefit best from a psychiatric and psychological evaluation and from having both medical and mental health professionals working closely with each other on the individuals' treatments. Although some stimulant medications can help control ADHD, they can have the side effect of increasing obsessive thoughts or compulsive behaviors. Strict monitoring of the medication's effects is necessary. Luckily, both ADHD and OCD can be successfully treated with behavioral therapy.

Is there a link between OCD and autism?

OCD and autism do share some characteristics, so it is important to really investigate the diagnostic criteria of the disorders. According to the *DSM-IV-TR* (2000), autism is characterized by significant impairment in social interaction (lack of appropriate emotional responses to events, such as not laughing at an event that most others would laugh at, or a lack of sharing enjoyment or interests with others), significant impairment in communication skills (delays in language development or the lack of make-believe or imaginative play), and repetitive and rigid patterns of behavior or interest (preoccupation with parts of objects or inflexible behavioral routines). One of these impairments must develop prior to the age of three for the diagnosis of autism.

Autism's delays in social development and language development are important to note; if a child is performing what appear to be rituals but also has delays in these areas, then autism is probably the appropriate diagnosis. However, if there are no delays in language or socialization, then OCD may be the more accurate reason behind the behaviors.

Is there a link between OCD and Asperger's disorder?

Asperger's and OCD share some commonalities. Asperger's is similar to autism (see previous question and answer), but without the lack of difficulty in language development. According to the *DSM-IV-TR* (2000), Asperger's is a developmental disorder that involves significant impairment in social interaction (such as minimal eye contact or a failure to develop social relationships) and repetitive or stereotyped patterns of behavior or interest. It is this second area where OCD and Asperger's can overlap.

However, there are ways to differentiate between the two disorders. People with Asperger's have a preoccupation with a certain subject or object that does not bring them distress—in fact, they often enjoy it. An obsession would bring someone with OCD distress. Second, although people with Asperger's do have routines that they follow with very little variation, the behavior is not done in response to an obsession. It's true that OCD can be diagnosed just based on the performance of inflexible routines not spurred by an obsession, but if this pattern of behavior is accompanied by difficulties in social interaction starting in early childhood, then Asperger's disorder is a better diagnosis. If there are no apparent difficulties in social interaction, then OCD may be the best diagnosis. Of course, it is possible to be diagnosed with both disorders as well.

Is major depressive disorder common in people with OCD?

Yes, major depressive disorder (MDD) can be a common affliction for people with OCD—research suggests that up to 80 percent of people with OCD also meet the criteria for the diagnosis of MDD at some time in their lives. Individuals could easily become depressed because of the interference of OCD in their life. Some individuals with OCD may even become suicidal, thinking that there is no way out of their spiral of obsessions and compulsions. Also, OCD and MDD can often be treated with the same medications, so there may be a relationship between OCD and MDD in the brain. In fact, medications for both disorders focus on serotonin, so even at a neurotransmitter level there may be a relationship between OCD and MDD.

In terms of treatment, severe depression can interfere with the treatment of OCD, especially with the motivation to do exposure therapy. Therefore, it is best to treat severe depression first, with either therapy or medications or with a combination of both. Once the MDD is brought to more moderate levels, then you can start therapy for the OCD, but it will be very important to watch for any signs of relapse of MDD, especially any thoughts or intentions of suicide.

Is worrying a part of OCD?

Yes, worry plays a major role in OCD; in fact, OCD has been called "the doubting disease." When we doubt things, we worry about the consequences of our actions, thoughts, or feelings or about the intentions or capabilities of others. Therefore, people start to worry in order to do one of two things:

1. If I worry hard enough, I can prevent bad things from happening. Many people have the mistaken idea that worrying about something

will somehow keep it from happening. How many mothers have worried about their son driving his car at night, only to think to themselves when he arrives home safely, "If I had not worried about him, something bad might have happened"? Yet, the son's driving played much more of a role in his safety than his mother's worrying did. This mistaken belief is exponentially worse in the minds of people with OCD.

To see if worries prevent anything from happening, do this simple task. Hold a pen in your hand over the floor and worry about the pen *not* hitting the floor when you let go of it. Then, let go of the pen and see what happens. If worries could prevent things from happening, the pen would have floated in the air. If you can't float a pen in the air by worrying about it, how will your worries prevent deaths, disasters, or other dreaded outcomes?

2. If I worry hard enough, I will be able to think of every bad thing that might happen, and if I can think of every bad outcome, then I can prepare for every bad outcome, and there will be nothing to worry about. People who try to worry about everything often do not enjoy anything because all they do is spend their time worrying. Or they think of so many bad things that might happen that they don't do much of anything at all, as a way to avoid the bad things they fear. So instead of enjoying the fact that their children are out playing with their friends, they may instead worry that the children will fall and get hurt or do something that will make all of their friends dislike them. Because of that fear, such parents with OCD may start to prevent their children from going out to play. Although this prevents their children from being hurt while playing or from offending their friends, it also prevents them from being kids and enjoying their childhood.

When people with OCD worry, they jump to the worst-case scenarios—the things that they fear the most. Because they are so focused on these extreme fears, they do their rituals to prevent the possibility of these things happening. However, worry is insidious—it just keeps coming back, and the worries return again and again, possibly leading to more compulsive behaviors. The goal of therapy is to break the link between the thoughts and behaviors, getting people to recognize that just because you think something does not mean it is true and that you need to do something to undo the thought.

How can coexisting conditions complicate OCD (or vice versa)?

The treatment of OCD can be made more difficult by the presence of other mental health disorders, and vice versa. For example, individuals with MDD and OCD may have to deal with the presence of suicidal thoughts in addition to obsessions and compulsions.

When OCD is diagnosed along with another disorder, it is important for any professional treating the disorders to prioritize and treat the more serious disorders first—for example, it would be best to deal with any suicidal thoughts before focusing on any OCD treatment. Then the therapist will have to come up with a plan to address all the symptoms in the most effective way, with therapy, medications, or a combination of both.

Because it is not uncommon to have more than one diagnosis, individuals with OCD need to work with their therapists and be honest about their symptoms, any medication side effects, and their willingness to potentially delay the treatment of their OCD so that another more serious diagnosis may be addressed first. On the other hand, if their OCD is making other disorders worse, then the OCD may initially need to be the main focus of treatment. A thorough diagnostic interview is necessary before the therapist and the person with OCD can come up with a definitive treatment plan. See Chapters 7 and 8 to review how to choose a therapist.

How can stress levels affect OCD?

Stress levels can play a large role in OCD; many individuals note that their OCD gets worse when they are under stress. This can lead to heightened obsessions or compulsions. People with OCD rely on their rituals as a way to manage stress. Of course, the stress can increase the chances of having the obsessions as well, so it can be a circular occurrence.

Stress can lead to experiencing more obsessive thoughts or an increase in their intensity. For example, if you hear a news story about a house being broken into, that can lead to obsessive thoughts about a burglar in your own home. That can increase anxiety, which in turn may lead to an increased chance of compulsive behaviors, such as checking locks or being sure that a burglar alarm is set over and over again. Of course, as the compulsions increase, a person can experience more stress as a result of lack of sleep because they keep checking the locks. That lack of sleep leads to more chances for the mind to wander, possibly leading to more obsessions, more anxiety, and therefore more compulsions.

Therapists, beyond just doing therapy with a person, may also offer some suggestions for stress reduction. Some easy ways to do this follow:

- Quit smoking. Smoking increases the heart rate, making the body work harder and leading to more potential for feeling on edge or keyed up.
- Stop drinking caffeine. Caffeine, similar to cigarettes, can lead to a general feeling of agitation.

- Exercise. Some daily exercise can have a natural stress-reduction effect because exercise naturally increases serotonin levels.
- Eat right. Comfort foods may feel good in the short run, but in the long run they lead to decreases in serotonin levels, as well as a chance for increased blood pressure caused by the excess weight that people may gain from eating that food.

What is obsessive-compulsive personality disorder?

Obsessive-compulsive personality disorder (OCPD) "is a preoccupation with orderliness, perfectionism, and mental and interpersonal control, at the expense of flexibility, openness, and efficiency" (DSM-IV-TR, 2000).

Individuals with OCPD want things done their way and only their way—they would rather take on an entire project on their own than delegate any part of it out to other people. They may hold onto money instead of spending it, in an Ebenezer Scrooge sort of fashion. People with OCPD would rather work than be with friends, would prefer to argue their points to make people believe them rather than engage in a friendly discussion, and are so focused on details that they often do not enjoy the activities that they do (they will only see flaws in a project instead of the fact that everyone else loves the work).

People with OCPD attempt to get a great deal of things done, but often, because they get so bogged down in the details and do not ask for help, they fail to meet deadlines or constantly seek extensions. At the same time, they get frustrated when people try to give them advice or if people get angry at them for not trying an "easier" way.

People with OCPD may also see themselves as having to be better than others, needing to take the high ground morally in all areas and seeing others who do not hold the same values as weak or below them. They are rigid, seeing only their way as the correct way.

What is the difference between OCD and OCPD?

People with OCD experience obsessions and compulsions, whereas people with OCPD do not, unless they also have OCD. People with OCD and OCPD can share traits, such as hoarding items, perfectionism, and scrupulous thoughts. However, OCPD is about a pattern of interaction with everyone and everything in the person's environment, whereas OCD is more related to specific fears or behaviors.

Although we often hear people jokingly telling their friends or loved ones that they have OCD, what is more likely is that they have traits of OCPD. If there is an identified, absolute result that a person holds firm to, but there are no obsessions related to it, and the person could perform any of several behaviors to get to that result, then the behavior is more likely related to OCPD than OCD. For example, a person with OCD may fear having a thought about wanting premarital sex. They may think that having that thought will make them more likely to perform the act and therefore anger God. Individuals with OCPD may just think that it is wrong, period—they have no fear of the thought or any inkling that having the thought will make them do it. Instead, they are likely to believe that anyone who does it is morally wrong, whereas people with OCD will generally judge only themselves and not anyone else. Some underlying traits of OCPD may be more common than people think.

Chapter 7

PSYCHOLOGICAL THERAPIES FOR OCD

- Can people be cured of OCD?
- Where can OCD patients get help?
- What is the difference between a psychiatrist and a psychologist, and how do they treat OCD differently?
- Are there people besides psychologists and psychiatrists who can help individuals with OCD?
- Who can diagnose OCD?
- What treatments are available for OCD?
- What is cognitive behavioral therapy (CBT)?
- I heard that Sigmund Freud coined the phrase "anal-retentive," which is often used to describe OCD. Do his theories still play a role in the treatment of OCD?
- What are cognitive distortions, and how are they related to OCD?
- Is there any research on what themes of thoughts typically maintain OCD?
- What is exposure and response prevention (ERP) therapy, and how does it work?
- Does ERP have any side effects?
- If I do exposure therapy, will the therapist make me do things I don't want to do?
- How successful are CBT and ERP?
- Do therapists use any kinds of technology in their therapy sessions?
- Is biofeedback a helpful treatment for OCD?
- Is systematic desensitization a helpful treatment for OCD?
- What role does choice play in fighting my fears?
- Are there things that I can do while performing an exposure to make it easier on myself?
- I've heard of hand washing and fear of germs, but that's not me; my OCD is different. Can treatment still work for me?
- What questions should I ask a therapist to be sure he or she knows how

to treat OCD?

- The thoughts and compulsions get so strong that I feel like I am out of control. How is it possible to implement therapy techniques when you can't control your thoughts or actions?
- How might I be able to tell if my therapist doesn't have the right experience with OCD to treat me effectively?
- What types of treatment are available for OCD?
- Can you be hospitalized for OCD?
- What does residential treatment for OCD consist of?
- What is a partial hospitalization program (PHP) for OCD?
- What is an intensive outpatient program (IOP) for OCD?
- What is traditional outpatient (TOP) therapy for OCD?
- What is the typical duration of treatment for OCD?
- Can OCD come back after I have been treated for it successfully?
- Will OCD go away on its own if I do not get any treatment?
- What if I start therapy but want to stop it after a few sessions?
- Are there some techniques that I can use on my own without having to see a therapist about my OCD?
- Are there any nontraditional or holistic therapies available for OCD?
- There really are bad and good events, and I know that I am right about this—will you try to change my belief system if I do therapy?
- Is there a model explaining OCD that CBT therapists follow?
- Using that model, how can a therapist help a person with OCD change?
- Is there a surgery to cure OCD?
- Can spirituality cure OCD?
- Does insurance pay for treatment?
- I believe that my OCD helps me to control my world—why would giving it up help me?
- What are some techniques to challenge OCD about physical health?
- Is there any type of OCD that can't be helped?
- Are there any testimonials I can read from patients who have been treated successfully in the past?

Can people be cured of OCD?

When discussing a mental illness, therapists do not use the word "cured." Cured implies a disease, and OCD is not a disease; it is a disorder. A disease is something that you catch, like the flu. You could go to the doctor and get some medication, and the flu would be gone in a few days. On the other hand, a mental disorder is a pattern of thinking and behaving that interferes in a person's daily life. In the case of OCD, people with OCD may know logically that washing their hands for two hours is excessive, but their fear of germs is so great that it overrides that logic and compels them to continue to wash. They may have felt this behavior was helpful to them when they started it, or it probably did not initially interfere greatly with their daily life. However, as time went on, and it got more out of control, the washing became harder and harder to stop and developed into a compulsion.

Therapy can help a person learn new ways to deal with obsessions and decrease compulsions, but that individual is making behavioral changes rather than being cured of his or her OCD. Medications (see Chapter 8) can help to alter the way a person's brain processes information, but that medication will not cure the person because once the person stops the medications, his or her chances for relapse are rather high, because psychotropic medications do not permanently alter the brain. A combination of therapy and medicine, or even therapy alone, can help drastically reduce and control the symptoms of OCD, but there is no way to permanently cure a mental disorder.

Where can OCD patients get help?

Individuals with OCD can find help from many different health care providers. Many people first seek assistance from their primary care physicians. Some of these physicians will prescribe medications, but many will refer their patients to a psychiatrist if their symptoms are difficult to treat. Psychiatrists will do a thorough interview with patients and then often prescribe medications as a first line of treatment for OCD. If the medications are helpful, then treatment will typically continue in that vein. However, if the symptoms continue to get worse, then a psychiatrist will typically refer the patient to a therapist who specializes in the behavioral treatment of OCD, and the two will work together to assist the patient.

Some people will start initially with seeing a therapist. Unfortunately, not all therapists specialize in the treatment of OCD, yet they still try to treat it—often unsuccessfully. It is important for anyone seeking treatment for OCD to ask if his or her therapist specializes in OCD.

Once a patient starts to work with a therapist, the process is exactly the opposite of the process begun with a psychiatrist; the therapist and patient design a treatment plan together to address the obsessions and compulsions. If there is not much progress, then a psychiatrist may be called in to consult on the case and possibly prescribe medication.

A place to seek initial help and get excellent information on how to find a doctor who is right for you is the Obsessive Compulsive Foundation, an organization for professionals who treat OCD and for people with OCD. They have a national conference every year and a website with a lot of great information: www.ocfoundation.org.

What is the difference between a psychiatrist and a psychologist, and how do they treat OCD differently?

Psychiatrists are medical doctors. They go to medical school and learn how to treat disorders from a medical perspective, meaning that they are trained in prescribing medications for people's problems. Psychologists go to graduate school and learn how to treat disorders using different types of talk and behavioral therapies.

Although some psychiatrists also do talk and behavioral therapy, and some psychologists are trained in evaluating medicinal effectiveness, most stick to their primary area of training. Both psychologists and psychiatrists are referred to as doctors. Psychiatrists, with their MD (doctor of medicine) or DO (doctor of osteopathy) degrees, are medical doctors, whereas psychologists, with PhD's (doctorate of philosophy), have doctorates in the philosophy of clinical psychology. There is also a new form of doctorate in psychology, called a PsyD, which is a psychology doctorate. The difference between a PhD and a PsyD is, in general, the focus of the training. The PsyD training has a focus on doing therapy, whereas the PhD training focuses both on doing therapy and on research.

The goal of both psychologists and psychiatrists is to help people who have mental disorders. Often, psychologists and psychiatrists work together on cases, with each handling his or her respective area of expertise—therapy or medication.

Are there people besides psychologists and psychiatrists who can help individuals with OCD?

Yes, there are many different types of mental health professionals. Individuals with master's or doctoral degrees in clinical psychology, social work, counseling psychology, community psychology, and even education can have training in treating OCD. Then there are the many people of varying levels of education who work underneath the doctors and other professionals.

Many students in different mental-health-based fields (e.g., psychology, social work, counseling, etc.) are required to do internships at various treatment sites and may also work with individuals with OCD. These students are often supervised by a doctoral- or master's-level trained clinician as a part of their education.

Some individuals in the education field can also specialize in mental health care and work with individuals with OCD. They may have an EdD (doctorate of education) or an MEd (master's of education). These individuals often work with school-age children and adolescents, but some also work with the general population.

There are also people in the medical field, such as primary care physicians and nurse practitioners, who can prescribe medications for individuals who are experiencing OCD symptoms. In fact, most individuals who are on medications for anxiety get their first prescriptions from their primary care physician, seeing a psychiatrist only if they need more specialized help.

No matter whom you may see about an OCD concern, just be sure that he or she is a licensed mental health professional. Some individuals call themselves therapists or counselors (depending on what state you live in, this can be legal to do) but have very little training in dealing with OCD.

Who can diagnose OCD?

OCD can be diagnosed by any of the professionals listed in the previous two questions who have a master's degree or higher, as long as they are licensed. All of these individuals have received specific training in the diagnosis and treatment of mental disorders. Again, just be sure to check that the therapist is licensed in the state that you are in or is working under the supervision of someone who is licensed.

Licensure assures that the therapist has had a specific level of training. Depending on the training or educational degree, therapists are required to take specific exams to assure their basic competence. These exams may be about specific treatments or disorders, basic knowledge of psychology, medication, or laws and ethics. Without passing these exams, a person cannot be licensed and therefore cannot practice without being under the supervision of someone who is licensed. Having someone who is licensed either administer your care or supervise and sign off on the work of your treatment provider can help ensure that your treatment is appropriate.

What treatments are available for OCD?

Several treatments are available for OCD. We explore these treatments in more depth in the following questions, but the main treatments are some form or combination of therapy, medication, or psychosurgery (brain surgery). Medication and therapy are the most widely available treatments for OCD; psychosurgery is in its infancy.

There is a debate in research literature about what works better—therapy alone or a combination of medication and therapy—but it does appear that both are about equally effective, with therapy alone having less relapse potential than a combination of therapy and medication.

Finally, some new areas involving brain surgery are being researched. Though still in their developmental stages, they may have some promising results for individuals with severe OCD. These surgeries are still in their experimental phases and are awaiting the approval of the FDA for full use.

What is cognitive behavioral therapy (CBT)?

Cognitive behavioral therapy (CBT) is the most researched form of mental health therapy there is. A basic facet of CBT is that therapists can use three things to understand their patients—the way people think, feel, and behave. Further, the goal of this therapy is to help people make changes in their behaviors, thoughts, and feelings.

CBT therapists have many ways to help their patients examine and challenge their thoughts. One is a thought record (see Appendix A). The thought record allows people to document and examine their thoughts, to see what types of distortions may exist, and to come up with ways to challenge these thoughts. Another technique is to challenge thoughts directly. If a patient says, "thinking something is as bad as doing it," the therapist may say something like, "I hope my car explodes today when I get into it." Then they may walk out to the therapist's car, and the patient can watch the therapist get into the car without it exploding, therefore challenging the notion that thinking something makes it happen. Or, a therapist may request that the patient convince the therapist that the patient is correct in his or her thinking. However, this often backfires on the patient, who begins to see that the therapist's challenges and questions to his or her way of thinking are more based in reality than the person's obsessions are.

CBT therapists also assist people in recognizing that experiencing a feeling does not mean that this is the only way that they can feel about the situation. For example, some people fear elevators, and other people enjoy them. But these feelings are not set—they can be changed. In fact, the person who fears the elevator may have enjoyed elevators until he or she got stuck in one a year ago. If a person's feelings can change from safety to fear, then it is possible for the feeling to return to safety again.

Finally, the focus is also on behaviors. A CBT therapist assesses what behaviors a person performs that could merit therapy. The therapist often suggests that a person modify his or her actions to get different results in his or her everyday life. For example, the therapist may do role-plays with a socially anxious person to teach that person new ways to interact with people, such as adding more eye contact, speaking louder, or not slouching.

Combining the areas of thoughts, feelings, and behaviors allows a CBT therapist to cover almost everything that can be a beneficial change for someone with OCD. Patients have a greater chance for success in dealing with their anxiety when all of these areas are targeted.

I heard that Sigmund Freud coined the phrase "anal-retentive," which is often used to describe OCD. Do his theories still play a role in the treatment of OCD?

"Anal retentive" is an outdated psychoanalytic term used to describe one of the stages of development in Sigmund Freud's theories. Prior to the research-based therapies that most mental health professionals use now, early—and unfortunately, some current—theories of psychology were based on people's own personal theories about why certain things happen to us instead of on science, facts, and quantifiable information. Freud is one of those psychiatrists who worked according to instinct instead of fact.

Freud devised a theory of personality development that was based on the effect of sexual pleasure on a child as he or she grows. This development came in five stages: oral, anal, phallic, latency, and genital. Freud believed that people could get "stuck" at a certain stage of development and that this had a profound effect on their adult personalities. He felt that individuals who fixated on the anal stage were very focused on their bowel movements and the retaining or releasing of their feces. He asserted that at this stage, the focus of the child (around ages two to four) is on the bowels: as toilet training occurs, the child has to decide whether he or she is going to hold his or her feces or release them. Because releasing feces is a source of pleasure for the child, he or she has to learn how to release it in the proper place at the proper time. Freud felt that children who had a very harsh toilet training learned that they had to suppress joy and pleasure in order to be accepted (going to the bathroom only when appropriate), and that they had to be perfect and exact in order to please people.

Most people age and master bowel control through training, but Freud felt it was possible to become developmentally stuck in this phase, transferring this perfectionism to other areas such as homework, organization, punctuality, and household chores. This was how Freud felt OCD developed. Unfortunately, this theory took hold and set back the treatment of OCD half a century, as was discussed in Chapter 1.

Today we call people who are particular about certain things "anal retentive" as a result of Freud's early theories. It may also describe people with OCD, but most individuals in the mental health field no longer associate this outdated terminology with OCD.

What are cognitive distortions, and how are they related to OCD?

"Cognitive distortions" is an umbrella term for certain types of thinking that are known to help maintain anxiety and depression instead of challenging them. There are many cognitive distortions listed in many books, with the most cited book probably being David Burns's *Feeling Good: The New Mood Therapy* (1999).

The cognitive distortions are as follows:

1. **Should statements:** You believe that there are such things that *should* be done and *shouldn't* be done, and you use these statements to beat yourself or others up when you or they do not meet expectations (I should have been perfect, or they should not have rearranged those items after I put them how I wanted them).

2. **Personalizing:** You blame yourself for anything that went wrong or any mistakes that were made, even if they were not your fault (Even though the firefighters said it was faulty wiring in the walls that caused the fire, I should have checked the outlets more carefully so that I could have discovered the problem and fixed it).

3. **Fortune telling:** You predict what the future will hold, often believing you know what others will think or feel about situations (If I do not wash my hands thoroughly enough, I will be seen as a dirty person, and I will get fired from my job).

4. **All-or-nothing thinking:** If it is not perfect, it is a failure (Even though 99 people gave me an excellent evaluation on my talk, one person said that it was only average, so I must have done a pretty horrible job).

5. **Rejecting the positive:** You pay attention only to the negative experiences because they are in line with what you believe, and you discount anything positive as an incorrect assessment (The one person who gave me an average evaluation on my talk was really the only person who was telling the truth).

6. **Emotional reasoning:** You believe that because you feel a certain way about something, it must be true (Even though everyone said they had a great time at the party, I know that they really didn't because I feel like I am just a failure as a hostess).

7. **Labeling:** You put yourself or others down for innocent mistakes (I am such a loser for taking that wrong turn—now I will not be early to the meeting like I should be).

These styles of thinking—which are very common if not ubiquitous in OCD—can have extremely negative consequences for people because they can maintain people's negative beliefs about themselves and the world. If all you can see is negative, then that is all that you will predict, and nothing will appear very positive. Therefore, it is important when working with a therapist to identify these thinking styles and to challenge them so that they will not interfere with the progress of treatment.

Is there any research on what themes of thoughts typically maintain OCD?

Yes, there is. The Obsessive Compulsive Cognitions Working Group (1997) noted that the most common thought themes found in OCD are the following:

- Responsibility: A person with OCD often believes that he or she is responsible for preventing bad things from happening.
- Uncertainty: Individuals with OCD believe as if they cannot tolerate uncertainty and that everything has to be absolutely clear.
- Perfectionism: An individual with OCD believes that everything must be perfect in order to avoid any form of critique from others. Or, she believes that she must do things perfectly in order to have a perfect life, or perfect knowledge, or perfect cleanliness, etc.
- Control: A person with OCD believes he must be in control of his thoughts and not think about anything bad or immoral, or have any intrusive thoughts at all.
- Thought Importance: The OCD belief that thinking something is almost as bad as doing it, or the belief that now that you have thought of something, it is more likely to actually occur. This is also referred to as Thought Action Fusion—thoughts are

somehow fused with actions, so if the thought occurs, the action must also occur.

- Dangerousness: A person with OCD believes that situations are far more dangerous or threatening than chance or probability would ever predict.

What is exposure and response prevention (ERP) therapy, and how does it work?

Exposure and response prevention (ERP) therapy, sometimes referred to as simply exposure therapy, is the treatment of choice in the professional literature and practice for helping individuals with OCD.

ERP is set up on a hierarchy, meaning patients work with a therapist to list all of their fears, and then they rank those fears from least to most anxiety-provoking. Starting with one of the lower-level fears, a therapist works with the person, and together they engage the feared experiences. So if a therapist is treating someone with OCD related to fears of contamination, they will work together to create a hierarchy about what "dirty" things are feared. After they make and rank that list, they will then go and expose themselves to the listed items (most ERP therapists will do this with their patients).

Let's say that touching the floor is a medium level of anxiety for a person because they feel that the floor is contaminated. A therapist will suggest to the person an exposure exercise and then get a level of anxiety from the person on a 0–10 scale; the therapist will then continue to assess the person's anxiety at frequent intervals during the exposure. They may start with kneeling on the floor and then sit on it. Next they may touch it with one finger, then two, then the whole hand, and then both hands, and so on until they are actually lying on the floor together. This may take an hour, or it may take twenty hours. Either way, the goal is to be constantly moving up the hierarchy to confront higher and higher levels of fear (see "Sample Hierarchy for Fear of Contamination" later in this answer).

Therapists hope to achieve a few things with ERP. First, they do not just expose a person to a situation and then run away—both patient and therapist have to stay in the situation until the person's anxiety is reduced to at least half of what it was when they started. This allows people to realize that they can do what they fear and see their anxiety decrease. Further, the individual needs to do this repeatedly—one time is not enough. The goal is to change a behavior, and it can take many repetitions before a new behavior is really ingrained. Doing an exposure also shows the patient that what he is doing is not really dangerous, since the therapist is willing to do it with him. If it really were dangerous, the therapist would not do it because it would be too much of a risk.

So ERP works by having people do what they fear, stay in the situation until they are no longer anxious or have reduced their anxiety level by half, and realize that just because they experience fear does not mean that anything bad will happen to them. Doing ERP can decrease compulsive behaviors by both inhibiting the rituals and challenging the validity of the obsessional thoughts.

Sample Hierarchy for Fear of Contamination

Low-level fears:
- Putting on shoes
- Picking up items that have been on the floor for under five seconds
- Seeing people sit on the floor
- Kneeling on the floor
- Walking on the floor with socks on
- Vacuuming the floor

Medium-level fears:
- Sitting on the floor, but not touching it
- Picking up items that have been on the floor for under twenty seconds
- Watching babies crawl on the floor
- Petting a dog that has been lying on the floor
- Touching the sides of shoes
- Touching the floor

High-level fears:
- Sitting on the floor and touching it
- Lying on the floor
- Picking up items that have been on the floor for more than twenty seconds
- Touching the soles of shoes

Does ERP have any side effects?

There are no medical side effects to ERP. Doing ERP does not have any known dangers other than chance; when doing an exposure, there will be times, based on chance, that things will go wrong. It is possible that while doing a driving exposure you will be in an accident. Or while doing an exposure based on not washing your hands, you may catch something and get ill. It is at these times that a person with OCD will likely have the greatest resistance to continuing the therapy and want to return to doing the rituals.

However, it's important for a person with OCD to remember that chance affects everyone equally. Good things and bad things happen to all of us, and doing a ritual will not prevent bad things from happening. In fact, it will lead to worsening OCD, which is obviously a bad thing. Therefore, it is important to recognize that doing ERP is a way to get you to think and behave almost like people without the disorder—to take risks and have fun and at times even be carefree. It also means accepting that things will happen to you by chance, just as they do to everyone else, and recognizing that you can handle these things, no matter what they are.

If I do exposure therapy, will the therapist make me do things I don't want to do?

No—no therapist can ever make you do anything you do not want to do. You are in control of your own therapy and have the final say in whatever it is that you do. However, many people are wary of going into therapy because they fear that they will be forced to do things that they are afraid of.

OCD specialists will work with you to design a hierarchy of your fears—ranking them from least to most fear-provoking. Then, starting at the lowest-level fears, they will work with you to move up the hierarchy. Therapists will continue to nudge you to challenge higher-level fears, but they will not force you to do something. If they do, it may be best to find a new therapist.

However, if you start to think a therapist is forcing you to do something, it may also mean that you are stuck, and you are perceiving their suggestions to move up your hierarchy as forcing you to do it. In addition to not forcing you to do anything, a therapist will not put you in any harm. Many therapists will do the things that you fear alongside of you to show you that they really are not dangerous. If these things were dangerous, then they would harm the therapist as well as you, and why would the therapist take that chance? So it would benefit you most if you would be willing to work with your therapist on a steady move up your hierarchy and be willing to do the things that you fear, even if you're uncomfortable at first. Recognize that your fear does not mean that anything bad will happen to you.

How successful are CBT and ERP?

Research shows that there is a 50 to 80 percent reduction in OCD symptoms over the course of 12 to 20 sessions of CBT and ERP treatment. That number of sessions may even be lessened if the treatment is performed in an intensive program, such as a partial hospitalization program or an intensive outpatient program (PHP or IOP). (See pages 144–145 for more information on these programs.) The best predictor for the success of the therapy is the patient's willingness to do the homework that is assigned by the therapist. Therapists are not responsible for their patients' improvement. Therapists are more like a coach than anything—they have the "plays," but the players need to execute the plays in order for the team to function. Similarly, the therapist can design a treatment plan and the exercises to do, but the patient has to do them in order to see improvement. Just like only playing a trombone at your music lessons will not increase your trombone playing ability very well, only doing exposures at the therapy session will also not be very helpful in fighting your OCD.

Do therapists use any kinds of technology in their therapy sessions?

There are some new technologies that can be helpful in the treatment of OCD, as well as some older technologies that are useful to this day. One burgeoning area being investigated is virtual reality (VR). VR can be helpful in assisting individuals who are initially fearful of trying to do an exposure. For example, if you have a fear of harming your child, then it could be possible for the therapist to first make a VR scenario of a child in a room, and you can walk into the room and play with the child. As time in the VR goes on, various things can be added to the room, such as a knife and a gun and a grenade, and so on. As these things are added, the person can test whether you would actually go and use one of these weapons and harm the child. Because people with OCD would likely be the last people to actually purposely harm someone about whom they have obsessions, you will learn that even with the means to harm your child, you will not do it. Then you can move on to actual exposures with your child (of course, it is not recommended to have military weapons around children because they might get a hold of them). Your exposures can involve sitting near your child or having your child in the kitchen with you while you are using a knife to slice food, and so on. This is a great way to use some modern technology to assist in therapy.

An older piece of technology that is still useful is tape players, or now, digital recorders. Many therapists have people write out the scenarios of what they fear and then record that onto a recorder. Then the person is to listen to that scenario over and over again until their anxiety about the scenario decreases. The goal is to start to realize that the scenario, which people often tend to try to suppress or avoid, is so out of the realm of possibility that there is no need to avoid it. Plus, as they listen to it, their fear of it actually decreases instead of increases.

One other recent technology tool is called telehealth. Telehealth is a camera and microphone system that can be used to record therapy sessions in remote locations. Rural hospitals or clinics need only a telephone line and some video equipment, and they can see and communicate with doctors in other locations to do therapy or to get consultations on therapy cases. As the technology improves, therapists will be able to reach more and more people in rural locations who may not have access to specialists in OCD.

Is biofeedback a helpful treatment for OCD?

Biofeedback is the process of receiving feedback about the condition of your body, often through the use of machines. Often, heart rate monitors or blood pressure monitors are hooked to computers so that live readouts can show what is happening with a person's body. For example, a person can be seated and hooked up to a biofeedback machine and asked to keep his or her heart rate under 70. If the rate goes above 70, a light may go on, and the person would have to try to relax enough to get the rate back below 70. Some therapists may then have patients think of their obsessions while trying to keep their heart rate down, showing them that they can remain calm even in the face of their obsessions.

Biofeedback has been shown to be excellent for pain management, especially headaches. Individuals can be trained to raise the temperature in their hands just by thinking about their hands getting warm, therefore drawing blood out of their head and into their hands, which leads to a decrease in pressure in the head.

Although biofeedback is a good therapy for pain and general stress management, this treatment modality is not recommended for OCD because OCD is more cognitively based (obsessions) than physically based. Plus, research shows that ERP is a far more effective treatment for OCD than biofeedback.

Is systematic desensitization a helpful treatment for OCD?

Systematic desensitization (SD), developed by Joseph Wolpe in the 1950s, is a form of therapy that attempts to pair two different response systems together—the fear system and relaxation. By having people do relaxation exercises and then think about gradually increasing anxiety-provoking situations based on their fear hierarchy, Wolpe attempted to have people decrease their anxiety by recognizing that they could remain relaxed even while thinking of the things they feared. By doing this, he was trying to extinguish the fear response to that thought.

SD is the forerunner to ERP therapy, which actually puts people into the situations that they fear in order to have them learn that they can handle the situations and that they do not need to run away from them. Therapists still use a modified version of SD in the treatment of OCD today when an exposure is hard or impossible to do (for example, if the fear is the death of a loved one, then that would have to be imagined instead of created) or when exposure may bring about such a high level of anxiety that it would be beneficial to imagine it before attempting it. We can thank Dr. Wolpe for being one of the people who helped to create the behavioral treatment of OCD and anxiety.

What role does choice play in fighting my fears?

There is nothing from an anxiety perspective that you cannot do. "Can't" is a choice when we are talking about OCD. If you say that you can do exposures to the floor, doorknobs, and shoes, but you can't touch a garbage can, you have just made a false statement— you can touch a garbage can, but you are choosing not to. If it were true that you couldn't touch a garbage can, the way the physical universe is viewed would have to be changed; you would be the only person in history who could touch anything but garbage cans. When we are talking about anxiety, there is no such thing as can't—there is only will you do it or won't you.

Plus, if you skip doing something in therapy, that means you are choosing to fear that thing, and that just does not make sense to do. Why would someone choose to face all of his or her fears but one? Skipping something is not a good option. Working with a therapist to break the exposure down into manageable parts would be the best solution for you to face anything you think you cannot.

Are there things that I can do while performing an exposure to make it easier on myself?

In the past, exposure therapy was combined with relaxation exercises or breathing techniques to teach people how to calm themselves in situations that they fear. However, this is being phased out of the most up-to-date treatment clinics because therapists and researchers have found that when people are focusing on relaxing, they are not focusing on doing the exposure as much as they could be, and the result is that the exposure has to last longer to be effective. However, if you are trying exposure on your own, relaxation techniques might be helpful in getting you through it at first, but you will want to move gradually toward exposures without the relaxation. If an exposure seems too hard, instead of distracting yourself from it with breathing techniques, it would be best to just break the exposure down into easier steps and do it that way. Then you are exposing to the fears without any kind of distraction.

Also, it may be beneficial to have someone who knows about your OCD check in on you. This will help keep you accountable to your own therapy. Also, be sure to write down the things on which you want to work. Sometimes just getting the obsessions out of your head and on paper can help to lessen their effect because once they are written, you can actually see how irrational many of them are. In your head, because you are so used to them, they may make perfect sense.

Finally, be true to yourself, in the sense that you will need to be serious about therapy. Saying things such as, "Today I will just do my rituals, but tomorrow I will go back to challenging them" is just going to make your OCD worse and will set you back. Be sure that you are always challenging the OCD, no matter what.

I've heard of hand washing and fear of germs, but that's not me; my OCD is different. Can treatment still work for me?

Yes, treatment can still work for you. Although hand washing and fears of germs and contamination are common OCD symptoms, OCD is not limited to these—OCD can take on many forms. However, movies and literature often associate OCD with fears of germs or contamination, so that is what most people are familiar with.

Rest assured that the treatment that works for the hand washing and germ/contamination-based OCD also works for the other presentations of the disorder. Treatment works on all forms of the disorder because the underlying mechanism in OCD is the same no matter what the presentation is—an overactivation of the Fight/Flight/Freeze (FFF) response. The goal of the treatment is to get to the heart of the trigger of the FFF response and to have people sit with that trigger without trying to undo it, allowing themselves to recognize that they can handle what it is that they fear. That is, treatment teaches sufferers to face their fear instead of trying to undo it with a compulsion.

What questions should I ask a therapist to be sure he or she knows how to treat OCD?

This depends on what type of treatment you are receiving or wish to receive. If you're looking for medication, it's important to be sure that you are seeing a psychiatrist. Although many general practitioners will prescribe psychiatric medications, you are better off seeing a psychiatrist who has had extensive, specific OCD training. However, if you are in an area of the country where there are no psychiatrists available, then a general practitioner will be fine.

If you're looking for a therapist, you want to make sure the therapist has specific training in OCD. If not, ask him or her to refer you to a therapist or psychologist who does. When you do meet a therapist who has OCD training, be sure that the therapist does exposure therapy. If he or she does not, then ask that therapist as well for a referral to another therapist, because the two empirically validated therapies for OCD are CBT and ERP. While other therapies might be helpful for OCD, none have been more researched than CBT and ERP.

The thoughts and compulsions get so strong that I feel like I am out of control. How is it possible to implement therapy techniques when you can't control your thoughts or actions?

Try this exercise. Take a ball and throw it in the air and catch it. Now, do the same thing, but think that you are going to miss it. Do not try to miss the ball; just think that you are going to miss it.

Even though you are thinking that you are going to miss, you still probably caught the ball. Therefore, just because you thought something bad (missing the ball) was going to happen, it did not actually happen.

The same can be said for OCD treatment. You may not feel you are in control of your thoughts, but this does not mean that you are unable to do anything to regain control. In fact, the initial goal of therapy is to get people to change their behavior even though they do not really believe 100 percent that it will change.

One of the major obstacles to OCD treatment is that people think they need to be in control of all of their thoughts and actions, and this is simply not true. If it were, then everyone would be hitting holes in one on the golf course (control of your actions), and no one would ever have a negative thought again. This will simply not happen, and it's OK. It's all about handling your reaction to inevitable negative thoughts, impulses, or images.

Remember this: you have never been, nor will you ever be, in total control of anything. To prove this, just try to stop blinking for the rest of your life. It is impossible. Once you can accept that, you will find it much easier to go and challenge things and accept that a lack of control is a reality for everyone, not just you.

How might I be able to tell if my therapist doesn't have the right experience with OCD to treat me effectively?

Not a lot of therapists are really very familiar with OCD, and unfortunately, some therapists inadvertently do more to make a patient *feel like* he or she is crazy than to help them. At a recent conference, a therapist was talking to a panel of experts about a patient she was treating. She was telling the experts about all of the terrible thoughts that the patient had when the experts stopped her and said that the thoughts were not terrible—they were just thoughts. She then started to argue with them, trying to convince them that the thoughts were terrible. Unfortunately, she had also conveyed to her patient that the thoughts were terrible, confirming for the patient that the poor guy was bad for having those thoughts.

But the thoughts were just thoughts—they were not good or bad. And people who have these thoughts are not crazy—they have OCD. If your therapist does not understand this, find another therapist. Search for an expert in OCD because an expert will understand how difficult these thoughts are for you—and how bad and guilty you already feel—and will be able to help you learn how to handle the thoughts.

What types of treatment are available for OCD?

Numerous types of treatment are available for OCD, either medical or psychological. The medical treatments can include surgeries and medications (see Chapter 8), and the psychological therapies can range from residential therapy, which can last for months, to traditional outpatient therapy, which is often once a week, or even less frequent. Please see the following questions for a full range of psychotherapy options for OCD.

Can you be hospitalized for OCD?

Yes, it is possible to be hospitalized for OCD. This can occur for several reasons. First, it may be a way to help stabilize someone whose rituals have become so problematic that all he or she does all day long is perform rituals. Often in these cases family members will bring someone in to a hospital because they do not know how else to get the person to stop ritualizing. This could happen because the person with OCD has reached out and asked for help that the family does not have the resources to give, or it could happen by force. At times, parents have just picked up their children and taken them to the hospital to get help. Or people with OCD may go to the hospital on their own because they are so overwhelmed by their OCD that they do not know where to turn to for help. Most likely the first step after the person reaches the hospital is the start of an intense medicinal intervention, followed by a transfer to some type of intensive outpatient treatment once the person is stabilized on their medications and has seen some decrease in his or her ritualizing.

Second, hospitalization could occur because of a medical complication that has resulted from the ritualizing (such as skin lesions from washing excessively or muscle cramping from bending over and retying shoes hundreds of times a day), or it may occur because a person is suicidal as a result of feeling ruled by their obsessions and compulsions. If this is the case, then the person should be stabilized in the hospital to be sure that he or she is not a danger to self, and then the person can be transferred to a less intensive level of treatment.

What does residential treatment for OCD consist of?

Residential treatment for OCD involves living at a treatment center for a period of time (typically one to three months) and participating in therapy daily. The typical day involves some group and individual therapy, as well as daily exposure therapy. A therapist is available 24 hours a day, so a person always has someone around if he or she needs immediate assistance or is in crisis. Psychiatrists are also available for medication consultations.

The goal of residential treatment is to immerse individuals with OCD into therapy. Typically, people who are going in for residential treatment have failed at lower levels of care. Therefore, they enter a residential facility and are monitored extensively. Also, their environment can be very controlled, such as through limitations on access to showers or hand washing or keeping certain areas off limits so that people cannot go back and check things.

Residential treatment can be very successful. The only drawback is that some people have real difficulties only at their homes or their jobs and do not have much difficulty anywhere else. Therefore, they may do well at a residential program, but still have problems when they go home. It is therefore crucial for residential programs to create exposures that will transfer to people's home environments to be sure that they are successful even after leaving the therapy.

What is a partial hospitalization program (PHP) for OCD?

A PHP is a six-hour-a-day treatment program usually based at a hospital or a clinic that treats OCD. Typically there will be some group work and some individual exposure work specifically focused on the

OCD. There may also be other treatment formats, such as art therapy groups, spirituality groups, medication management groups, and other groups focused on depression, codependency, and so on. All of these groups meet over the course of six hours a day, five days a week (depending on how your state and insurance carriers define PHP treatment, it may be a bit different in your area), and then the patient returns home for the night. In PHP, a patient also has access to a psychiatrist for medication consultations.

The goal of a PHP is, of course, to specifically address the OCD difficulties and other troubles, such as depression, that may be related to OCD. The treatment team consists of numerous professionals, such as psychologists, psychiatrists, nurses, and therapists. PHP is used either to assist people as they step down from inpatient care and slowly reenter their everyday lives or to give people who have not needed inpatient care but do require a significant amount of therapy a chance to get the help they need.

What is an intensive outpatient program (IOP) for OCD?

An IOP is similar to a PHP, but it lasts only three hours a day for a minimum of four days a week (again, subject to your state laws and insurance requirements, this may differ slightly in your area). In an IOP for OCD, most of the group work not specifically focused on OCD is eliminated, and the focus is mainly on doing ERP and CBT. During an IOP, you may be working on your exposures at the hospital or clinic, or you may even leave the building to work with your therapist in the environment where you experience your fear. For example, if you perform rituals surrounding checking the locks on your car doors, you and your therapist may go out to the parking lot and actually have you lock the doors once and then walk away from the car without going back to check and make sure that they are locked.

IOP programs are a good step-down from a PHP program and are also useful if a person requires more intensive therapy than can be provided in a traditional outpatient therapy (typically once-a-week therapy appointments) setting, but does not need the intensity of a PHP. Psychiatrists are still able to consult with their patients while they are in an IOP level of care.

What is traditional outpatient (TOP) therapy for OCD?

TOP for OCD can be maintenance therapy for someone who has stepped down from an IOP level of care, or if a person does not require a higher level of care, it could be the only type of therapy he or she needs. Most people are familiar with TOP from television shows or movies with scenes showing therapy sessions (though most of the time the therapists are portrayed as unethical dolts who either sleep with their patients or have no idea how to help them). In TOP sessions, therapists work on exposures with their patients, assign homework exposures for their patients to do, and assess how their patients are performing in their daily lives, giving advice if needed or acting as a sympathetic ear in other instances. As time goes on, the sessions can be spaced out over the course of weeks or months until a person sees his or her therapist only on an as-needed basis.

A typical TOP session lasts forty-five to fifty minutes. The first session usually involves a lot of paperwork and an interview to get any pertinent background information (such as history of OCD symptoms), as well as establish a diagnosis. Subsequent sessions involve reviewing how things went in the last week—what stressors occurred, how many times a person experienced obsessions or compulsions, and how he or she challenged these. Then, the therapist may have the person do some exposures in the session, or they may go together to do some exposures in public. Finally, the therapist will assign some homework for the patient to do before the next session.

What is the typical duration of treatment for OCD?

That will depend on the severity of the OCD. Some residential treatment centers average thirty to sixty days of treatment, with step-downs first to PHP (six hours of treatment each day) and then to IOP (three hours of treatment a day) programs for several more weeks, leading finally into TOP, which can last for a few months to a year or more. There is no standard recommended time frame for therapy for OCD because each patient has a different presentation.

If a person is on medication for his or her OCD, then in a typical trial he or she will remain on the medication for at least six months, but more typically a year, and then attempt to taper off of the medication. It is important to do this slowly. If, along the way, the symptoms return, the dosage can be increased, and it may be recommended that a person remain on the medication for several years before again attempting to taper off. And, some people will be on medication for the rest of their lives.

Can OCD come back after I have been treated for it successfully?

Unfortunately, OCD can return after it is successfully treated—remember, OCD is never cured. However, there are ways to help keep OCD at bay once the symptoms have been eased because of treatment. First, if you have been prescribed medications, be sure to take them according to your doctor's instructions. Some medications can have very bad side effects or consequences if they are stopped too quickly, so be sure to make any medication changes in conjunction with advice from your doctor.

If you have successfully completed therapy, it may be beneficial to set up booster appointments every three to six months or so just to check in with your therapist and ensure that things are going well. Just knowing that you are going to see your therapist again may be enough of an incentive to practice the skills that you learned in therapy—it keeps you accountable for your own health and wellness. Further, if you did exposure therapy, it benefits you to continue to do exposures to challenge your fears and to build on the skills that you learned in therapy.

Will OCD go away on its own if I do not get any treatment?

Most likely not, but in rare cases OCD will go into remission and never come back. Science can explain why this happens in some cases and not in others. Sometimes these are referred to as miracles because there is no known psychological or medical reason for the change (there is a reason for the change, however, we are just not yet advanced enough to know what it is).

Though spontaneous remission is not unheard of, it is extremely rare and not something to wait around for. If you have the symptoms of OCD, your best move is to find a therapist who specializes in CBT and ERP and start therapy right away.

What if I start therapy but want to stop it after a few sessions?

This is very common; many people consider quitting therapy at some point during their treatment. There are many reasons—the cost, not seeing results quickly enough, fear of doing exposures, side effects of medication, or just difficulty with time commitments.

But whatever the reason or excuse, it is always best to stick with treatment. If you are not pleased with your therapist, you can always ask for a recommendation for another, but just stopping therapy altogether is very rarely helpful. As well as stalling the process of dealing with obsessions and compulsions, it may even make it harder for you to get help in the future because you may decide there is no need to return to get treatment given that it was not really helpful in the past anyway.

The effectiveness rate for therapy, especially ERP, CBT, and medications, is very high, and if those don't sound like treatments that you are interested in, there are numerous other therapies available that may help your OCD. One of these is bound to work, as long as you give it a fair chance. Staying in therapy even through the uncomfortable or even painful moments may be the only way for you to ease the symptoms of your OCD.

Are there some techniques that I can use on my own without having to see a therapist about my OCD?

If you suspect you have OCD, seeing a therapist is recommended, but there are several techniques that you can use on your own to start challenging your obsessions and compulsions:

- Ask yourself this question—would I tell my best friend to perform this compulsion to get rid of an obsessive thought, or would I tell my friend to just forget about it and go on with his or her day? Most likely you would tell this friend to just go on with his or her day. Follow the advice that you would give to someone else in the same situation and see what it is like to handle it without a compulsion.
- Delay your ritual; try starting with a few seconds and going from there. As time goes by, you may recognize that if you can delay

the ritual for several minutes, then there may be no reason to even do it at all.

- Try to streamline your ritual. Make a list of the steps involved, and then start to eliminate some of them. As you do this, you will decrease the amount of time spent ritualizing.
- Encourage individuals who have helped you to do rituals to slowly pull back from helping you. This will lead you to be more responsible for your behavior and will reduce your reassurance-seeking.
- Plan an opposite day. Take one day and do the opposite behavior of your normal ritualizing just to see if anything negative actually happens.

These tips can help you start to degrade the strength of the rituals and the obsessions that cause them. Although you should probably also seek therapy, these are excellent starting points.

Are there any nontraditional or holistic therapies available for OCD?

There are some therapists who use different types of nontraditional treatments to treat OCD. Many of these are labeled "expressive therapies" because they are focused on ways of expressing stress and healing through mediums other than words.

In dance/movement therapy (D/MT), the therapist's goal is to assist the OCD individuals in developing greater self-awareness through a clear sense of how their mind and body interact. Therapists can do this by having individuals identify their emotions, thoughts, feelings, and perceptions and then see which reactions are provoked by certain physical situations. D/MT therapists focus on body language to gauge a person's fears and then try to create a safe physical situation in which that person can heal. The therapist hopes to help people learn to tolerate and "move through" their stress instead of escaping from it. The techniques can include breathing exercises, yoga, relaxation, or even Tai chi. The therapist then helps the patient express and address future needs through movement and words.

Through art therapy, people can draw their problems to help them separate from their anxiety. Through their drawings, they can explore their fears and face them in a safe manner, which teaches them that they can handle their fear. They can also draw themselves interacting with their fears in new ways, as a way to explore how they hope to act when they are able to handle their fears.

Puppet therapy uses puppets as models of people and can help to access the playful side of the patient. Through the use of the puppets, therapists can model new behaviors. Then the patients can try those behaviors with the puppets prior to trying it themselves, so that they have a way of acting on the behaviors before performing them in real life.

Some therapists use techniques from Eastern medicine, such as acupressure on the forehead and the back of the head. It is hoped that through pressure on certain acupuncture points and through the person's taking deep breaths, the intensity of the thoughts or emotions will decrease and be replaced with calm emotions.

Any of these therapies could be used in conjunction with ERP, CBT, or medication to treat OCD.

There really are bad and good events, and I know that I am right about this—will you try to change my belief system if I do therapy?

A worthwhile therapist would never try to change your moral or ethical belief system in therapy. However, therapy may be a challenge if you really do believe that your way is the only way to look at the world. Therapists attempt to help people change the way they perceive things. Almost everything is neutral—there is no one thing in the world that everyone is afraid of, and there is no one thing in the world that everyone loves. However, there are many perceptions about everything. Take an elevator, for example. Let's say that standing in front of an elevator are a four-year-old girl who loves to push buttons and her fifty-year-old grandfather, who has an elevator phobia. When the doors open, the girl will want to run in and push the buttons, whereas her grandfather will not want to get in. How can the elevator be both fun (for the girl) and frightening (for the grandfather) at the same time? Well, the elevator is really neither fun nor frightening. It is a neutral object and purely subject to the perception or opinion of anyone who interacts with it.

So, therapists will try to work with you to change the way you perceive certain things, but they will not tell you that you need to modify your ethical code.

Is there a model explaining OCD that CBT therapists follow?

There are models of OCD that therapists follow, and a simple one is as follows:

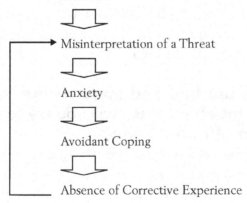

Situation

Misinterpretation of a Threat

Anxiety

Avoidant Coping

Absence of Corrective Experience

Let's walk through the model. First, an event or emotional experience occurs and triggers an obsession. For someone without OCD, this situation is probably no big deal, but a person with OCD tends to find ordinary situations threatening. In order to deal with the resulting anxiety, many people with OCD want to run away when it happens or avoid it altogether.

For example, there are people who suffer from obsessions about harming others. They may think to themselves, "I wonder if I punched the bus driver when I got off the bus?" They would become anxious, thinking that they might have harmed someone. Or they will want to make sure they did not do anything harmful so they can alleviate (avoid) the feelings of anxiety they are experiencing. Therefore, they might want to run after the bus to see if they harmed the driver, or they may go home and listen to the news to see if there are any reports of bus drivers being attacked by passengers. Although this ritual may lead to that quick feeling of relief, it also prevents them from learning that they could have handled the situation by sitting with the thought and recognizing it as an obsession. Instead, they inadvertently confirmed that the obsession could have been true and that they are safe only because of performing the ritual. Therefore, the next time the situation presents itself, they will be more likely to avoid it or seek reassurance to feel safe instead of facing it. This is how OCD behaviors are maintained.

Using that model, how can a therapist help a person with OCD change?

Looking at the model from a CBT perspective, there are three areas on which to focus. The misinterpretation of the threat is the *thought*, the anxiety is the *feeling*, and the avoidant coping or reassurance-seeking is the *behavior*. Because it is almost impossible to change a feeling without first doing anything else, we will not want to start there (just tell yourself to never be stressed again and see if it works). It is a bit easier to help a person change the way he or she thinks about things, but that is also rather difficult to do and takes some time (try convincing White Sox fans that the Cubs might actually win the World Series someday, and see if they will ever believe you). So we are left with the behavior, which is actually the easiest place to intervene—a person does not have to feel that things are fine or think that everything will turn out all right in order to still perform a behavior. Once the behaviors are changed, hopefully the thoughts and feelings will follow.

Consider this example. Chris, Tony, and Rob all go to the carnival. Chris and Tony ride the roller coasters (situation). Rob does not want to ride the roller coasters because he thinks they are dangerous; if he gets on the roller coaster, it might break (misinterpretation of a threat), which makes him afraid (anxiety), so he does not ride them (avoidant coping). Even though his friends are teasing him, he is convinced that he is safe because he's not on a roller coaster (absence of a corrective experience). Soon, however, Courtney comes up to Rob and asks him to ride the roller coaster. Rob has had a crush on Courtney for years, and he now finds himself in a bind: he thinks the roller coaster is dangerous, and he is anxious, but he does not want to appear afraid in front of Courtney, so, to hopefully win her heart, he rides the roller coaster with her, and he actually enjoys it.

The only thing he changed was his behavior, but by doing that, he had a corrective experience—he learned that there is not a 100 percent likelihood that riding on a roller coaster will harm him. Therefore, he will now have to change the way he thinks about roller coasters, and his anxiety will therefore decrease. He will have to do this behavior several times to get the full effect and to avoid seeing this one instance of safety as just pure luck, but once he does more of these exposures to what he fears, he will be able to see a decrease in both his threatening thoughts and the resulting anxiety.

Is there a surgery to cure OCD?

Surgery is reserved for the most difficult cases of OCD—those that fail to improve after all possible nonsurgical treatments, such as medications, behavioral therapy, and so forth. The goals of surgery are to make patients more functional and independent, to improve the symptoms of OCD, and, in most cases, to decrease the need for medications, particularly if the medications' side effects are problematic. In the past, the most common procedures (capsulotomy, anterior cingulotomy) involved making small lesions in the deep brain structures, such as the cingulate gyrus, the anterior capsule, or other areas of the brain that participate in the limbic system (the fear center of the brain) and its connections. This was done using either high frequency radio waves or with thin wires that had electrodes on them which would burn small portions of brain tissue. These procedures were done with special guidance from information gleaned pre-surgery using computed tomography (CT scan), magnetic resonance imaging (MRI), or other brain scans or testing.

Two main issues are related to the risk of surgery: the destruction of important areas of the human brain and the irreversibility of surgical effects. Older surgical procedures required cutting through healthy parts of the brain, or snaking wires through the brain to the disordered areas, which could also damage the healthy parts.

Currently, the two most promising trends include either making brain lesions with stereotactic radiosurgery (using, for example, a gamma knife) or implanting special deep-brain stimulators that modify brain activity like the lesions do, but without actual destruction of brain tissue. Radiosurgery, such as with a gamma knife, does not require any incisions and is done on an outpatient basis, making it very attractive for those who want to avoid staying in the hospital. However, even though no instruments are used, radiosurgery, which is also irreversible, still destroys small areas of the brain; the gamma knife does this by directing a beam of radiation at a certain point in the brain without damaging parts of the brain around that point or, amazingly, damaging any of the tissue the radiation must pass through to get to that point.

Deep brain stimulation, on the other hand, does not destroy any tissue, and therefore its effects are reversible as well as adjustable, given that the stimulation may be changed depending on the patient's response. The procedure of stimulation, however, is more involved and requires implantation of pacemaker-like devices (battery packs) and insertion of electrodes into the brain. Once the devices are in, a clinician can cause the stimulators to create electrical charges, affecting certain nerves in the brain and having an effect on a person's thoughts, anxieties, and behaviors. As stimulation increases or decreases, obsessions and compulsions can be measured to see if they increase or decrease. The stimulation can be altered until, theoretically, a person has no, or almost no, OCD symptoms. Both of these approaches are done primarily in major research and clinical centers; large-scale investigations are currently underway to determine which surgical approach is safest and most effective.

Can spirituality cure OCD?

There is no evidence that suggests spirituality can cure OCD. And, as noted in past questions, therapists do not really talk about curing OCD as much as learning to live with and handle it. Although there have been some recent discussions in the media about the positive effect prayer has on healing, the most recent study (Study of the Therapeutic Effects of Intercessory Prayer (STEP) by Benson, et al. (2006)), shows that there may actually be a negative impact on health when people know that they are being prayed for. So, there is no conclusive evidence in either direction about whether spirituality can be helpful in overcoming OCD.

That said, the best way to work toward improvement is having belief in yourself and faith that you can improve and that your OCD will not be in control of you. This belief can be a touchstone to help you push through your therapy exercises and deal with any setbacks that you may have along the way. If you approach therapy with a positive attitude, you have a better chance of seeing improvement; if you think that therapy will not work for you, you will most likely encounter treatment failure.

Does insurance pay for treatment?

That really depends on the type of insurance you have and what your benefits are. Insurance typically covers individual therapy sessions, which are generally weekly. People usually have some type of inpatient coverage available to them as well. It can be harder to get coverage when the services are for intensive therapy programs (either PHP or IOP). It can be even more difficult to get coverage for residential therapy because of the costs—it can cost between $20,000 and $40,000 per month for twenty-four-hour residential coverage for OCD. As with most insurance plans, there will probably be some out-of-pocket expenses, which could include deductibles or even full payment if your insurance coverage is denied.

The process of getting insurance to cover your treatment can be tricky—many things could cause or result in denial of coverage. First, if a company believes that your OCD is a preexisting condition from prior to when you joined them, they can deny coverage for the OCD treatment. Second, they may limit the amount of coverage that you can use, opting for a less intensive form of treatment than what is being recommended. Third, if the hospital or clinic somehow makes a mistake on a bill, the company can deny coverage and bill you instead. You will then need to talk to the clinic's billing department and get them to re-submit the bill correctly. Also, there are often limits on mental health coverage in insurance plans, so check with your insurance company before starting any therapy to find out how much coverage you have (such as number of sessions covered, amount of deductibles, or amount of co-payments).

Needless to say, this can be a difficult process. Most treatment centers will take the time to assist you with getting coverage for your treatment, but that is a courtesy. The bottom line is that it is your responsibility to know what your coverage is.

A current focus in Congress is mental health parity, which means making a law that will require insurance carriers to have the same benefits available for everyone for both mental and physical health. Currently, physical health benefits are superior to benefits for mental health on most insurance programs.

I believe that my OCD helps me to control my world—why would giving it up help me?

That sense of control you have is an illusion. All OCD helps you to control is your OCD through the relief you feel by performing compulsive behaviors over and over again. When that relief occurs, it feels as if you have averted an uncomfortable feeling or a dire consequence (such as keeping someone alive because you counted to 10). This relief is only temporary, though, because the obsessions often return. If OCD really did allow you to control things, then you would need to perform the ritual only once and then never need to do it again because then you would have established control, and there would be no need to reestablish it.

Also, if OCD really did help people to control their world, then we would all want to have OCD. Of course, this would bring about chaos because person A would want to control the world in his or her way, whereas person B would want to control it in an entirely different way. This would just not work. So, OCD does not actually help you to control anything. In fact, your OCD is probably in control of you more than you are in control of it. If you want to have a true sense of control, do what you can to eliminate your OCD, and then see what life is like not being controlled by a mental disorder. This will probably feel much better than always following the rules of your OCD.

What are some techniques to challenge OCD about physical health?

The OCD treatments we have already discussed—therapy (CBT and exposure, or ERP), medications, or a combination of the two—can be effective ways to treat fears of physical health. Education is also very important. Teaching people about appropriate hand washing is often necessary (no more than thirty seconds, or else you start to damage the oils on your hands and eventually your skin, leading to a greater chance of contamination in the future). It is helpful to have a nurse provide this education because nurses are experts in this area. Also, some basic education about viruses and germs can be helpful (for example, HIV only lives for about thirty seconds outside of the body). Once people with OCD have the right information, instead of focusing on what their obsessions tell them, such as "I can catch HIV if I touch a doorknob that someone with HIV touched within the last twenty-four hours," they may be more likely to challenge their obsessions.

Finally, a cost-benefit analysis of the OCD may be important. While it may appear that the benefits of the OCD are high (not getting ill due to a constant watch over your physical health), the costs are probably greater (alienating family members, for example, due to your always thinking that something is physically wrong with you), even though they may not be as readily apparent as the preceived benefits.

Is there any type of OCD that can't be helped?

There is no known OCD obsession or compulsion that is impervious to CBT, ERP, medications, or surgery. However, there are individuals who have not gotten much assistance from any of these forms of treatment, yet there is no clear theme of obsessions or compulsions that goes across the board for these individuals. OCD treatment is effective and helps most people who seek it out if they are willing to stick to the treatment. However, there will be individuals that will struggle with therapy. Therefore, instead of looking for a type of OCD that may be impervious to treatment, it may be better to search for personality traits that make accepting or responding to treatment more difficult. Or, brain scanning and imaging may, in the future, lead us to further understandings of why certain individuals have difficulty with treatment.

Are there any testimonials I can read from patients who have been treated successfully in the past?

Here is a testimonial from a person who recently completed an OCD PHP:

> When I came into [the] therapy program, I was hopeless. I had been at a behavioral health center for a week already being treated for depression, anxiety, and OCD, and my problems had only gotten worse. I had not been able to go to work because I was unable to sleep at night, and I was having panic attacks a

few times a day. I had also stopped eating and had lost almost fifteen pounds in three weeks. My case manager saw that I was not benefiting from the mood disorder program that I was currently in and decided to move me to a program that worked specifically with OCD and anxiety related disorders.

On my first day of treatment I was extremely optimistic. I was willing to try anything in order to feel better, even the exposure therapy that, at the time, seemed like cruel and unusual punishment. I sat down with my new case manager and explained to him that I had thoughts and memories that I could not stop thinking about. With anything that I saw or did, my mind would try to relate it to the specific thoughts and memories that I was trying to avoid. In my previous treatment, they tried teaching me to stop my thoughts and "just think of something else." Anybody who has OCD knows that they cannot "just stop" whatever it is that they have OCD about. Not to mention that when I could not "just stop" my thoughts, I became more concerned that there was something wrong with me, and I also feared the thoughts more and more. I told my case manager all of this, and he said it made perfect sense. For a moment I thought I had misunderstood him, but he explained to me that we cannot "just not think about something. That would be like saying don't think of a pink elephant. Whatever you do, don't think of a pink elephant," he said. Well, of course, I thought of a pink elephant. This was the first time in a week that I had felt like I was not going crazy and that there might actually be help for me.

For the next two weeks I worked with my case manager, and he had me do exposure therapy. He would have me compose a list of all of the things that I was afraid of or did not want to think of. Next, I would either write about those things or think about them for a couple hours. The point of this was to desensitize the thought or memory and have myself realize that it was simply just a thought, and it was not going to hurt me. After a few hours of thinking about these things, my body would slowly become less and less anxious. Eventually I got so used to thinking about certain things that I simply did not think about them anymore, because I was not trying to fight them. More and more time would pass before I would even realize that the thoughts that had been previously troubling me so much had been absent for large amounts of time.

In total, I spent two weeks in the OCD program. By the end of the two weeks I was able to sleep at night, eat again, go back to work—I had even stopped having panic attacks! Had it not been for the OCD program and the exposure and cognitive behavioral therapy, I can honestly attest that I would not be able to write this today, as I do not feel I would have ever recovered. Although there are times now when I may remember one of my thoughts that I was afraid of, and I may get slightly anxious, because of the program I now know not only how to, but that I *can*, handle my OCD.

Chapter 8

THE "OCD BRAIN" AND MEDICATIONS

- Is there a drug that is generally prescribed to all OCD sufferers?
- How often will I have to see a psychiatrist if I am using medications for treatment of my OCD?
- What is a neurotransmitter?
- What is the limbic system?
- What is serotonin?
- What is dopamine?
- What is norepinephrine?
- What is GABA?
- What is the difference between a neurotransmitter and an inhibitor?
- What are SSRIs, and how do they help treat OCD?
- Are there side effects to SSRIs?
- What are the names of some SSRIs that have been used to treat OCD?
- What are tricyclic antidepressants, and how do they help OCD?
- Are there side effects to tricyclics?
- What are the names of some tricyclics that have been used to treat OCD?
- What are MAO inhibitors (MAOIs)?
- What are the side effects of MAOIs?
- What are the names of some MAOIs that have been used to treat OCD?
- What are benzodiazepines?
- What are the side effects of benzodiazepines?
- What are the names of some benzodiazepines that have been used to treat OCD?
- What are neuroleptics?
- Are there side effects to neuroleptics?
- What are the names of some neuroleptics that have been used to treat OCD?
- What is D-cycloserine?
- Can you treat OCD with medications alone?

■ Once you start the medications, is it a lifelong commitment?
■ What if I cannot afford the medications for my OCD?
■ Is illegal drug use a problem for people with OCD?

Is there a drug that is generally prescribed to all OCD sufferers?

Many medications have been used for OCD. Some medications that were originally developed for depression also appear to have some positive effects on OCD. Medications that were developed specifically for anxiety also have been prescribed for OCD. The following questions and answers go through what medications are available for OCD, along with what side effects may be associated with each of these medications.

Further, keep this in mind—many of these medications take several weeks to reach their most effective treatment levels. Therefore, if you are going to use medications to treat your OCD, you need to commit to several weeks of taking the medication before you may feel that it is beneficial.

How often will I have to see a psychiatrist if I am using medications for treatment of my OCD?

The frequency with which you need to see a psychiatrist on an outpatient basis will depend on whether you are just starting on medications or have already been on them. The initial session with a psychiatrist, which will last around an hour, mostly gives the psychiatrist a chance to get a good history of your illness and then talk to you about what medications are available to treat your OCD. The psychiatrist will then give you a prescription for a medication and will probably want to see you two to three weeks later to be sure that there are no complications. Future sessions will probably be monthly or bimonthly for the first six months and will last approximately fifteen minutes each, just to see how the medication is working and to make any necessary adjustments. After you have been stabilized on a medication, you may meet with the psychiatrist every four to six months for prescription refills and any minor changes that may be needed. Of course, if there are ever any complications, you may call and make an appointment as needed.

What is a neurotransmitter?

Entire textbooks have been written about this question, so keep in mind that this answer will be very simplified. A neurotransmitter is the basis of all communication in the brain. Our neurons (the nerves in our brains) are not actually connected to each other. This is actually a good thing—imagine if your nerves were connected, and you cut your finger. There would be a direct line of pain running from your finger to the pain center in your brain, and there would be no way to shut the pain off. But because there are spaces between the nerves, our brain can place endorphins into the spaces (synapses). Endorphins are the body's natural painkillers, and they can buffer the transmission of the pain signals between the nerves. If that is not enough, we can take other pain medications (analgesics) to help decrease the pain. They too help block the transmission of pain signals between the nerves.

Therefore, because your neurons do not actually touch each other, they need to send messages to each other in order to communicate. They do this by using neurotransmitters. One neuron sends out neurotransmitters into the synapse between the nerves. When the neurotransmitters fill that space, they bounce onto the membrane of the next nerve. When this occurs, small electrical charges are generated, and when there are enough charges, an action potential (large charge) is created. This action potential allows for a message to be sent on to the next neuron. This process repeats itself again and again as the message travels from where it started to where it ends. One major area of current research focuses on how these neurotransmitters are related to the development and maintenance of OCD. Also being investigated are medications that can boost the workings of neurotransmitters that may have an influence on decreasing OCD.

What is the limbic system?

The limbic system is the part of the brain that regulates emotion and memory. It is located in the midbrain, which, from an evolutionary perspective, is the second oldest part of the brain (the brain stem is the oldest part, and the cortex, that wrinkly part of the brain, is the newest part). The midbrain is also sometimes called the reptilian brain because it is similar to the brain structure of reptiles, who do not have a cortex. The cortex grew around the midbrain and is what gives us our higher-order levels of thinking (processing math, reading, and so on).

Anxiety occurs in the midbrain, specifically in the limbic system. Therefore, the medications that target anxiety have some effect on the midbrain and the neurotransmitters there. We next review different neurotransmitters and how those medications affect them.

What is serotonin?

Serotonin is a neurotransmitter that has been linked to such functions as sleep, mood, and anxiety. Serotonin is synthesized in the body from tryptophan, a chemical that occurs naturally in food (there is a lot of tryptophan in turkey, which is why you often want to sleep after Thanksgiving dinner—pure tryptophan has a sedative quality). Medications that specifically increase serotonin levels have been shown to have a positive effect on the reduction of OCD symptoms.

What is dopamine?

Dopamine is a neurotransmitter, like serotonin, that may also be related to the development and maintenance of OCD. Current studies are investigating the role of dopamine alone, along with its interaction with serotonin, to see just how the two chemicals together impact OCD. At this point, it is impossible to say exactly how any specific brain chemical exactly impacts OCD.

What is norepinephrine?

Norepinephrine is a neurotransmitter found in high concentrations in an area of the brain called the locus coeruleus (LC). It has been found that the LC is related to the development and maintenance of OCD. Abnormalities in the neurons that utilize norepinephrine are linked to mood and anxiety disorders. Therefore, medications that focus on increasing norepinephrine have a positive effect on OCD.

What is GABA?

GABA is a neurotransmitter that is an inhibitor in the brain—it prevents action potentials from occurring. When people are anxious, many of their neurons in the fear center of their brain get excited (fire rapidly). GABA is a suppressor of those neurons. There has been a class of drugs developed specifically to affect the GABA system and help it to increase its inhibitory effects on the brain so that people will feel calmer and less anxious.

What is the difference between a neurotransmitter and an inhibitor?

This question is a bit tricky, but the simplest answer is that neurotransmitters are the chemical transmitters in the brain. Drugs are typically designed to increase certain neurotransmitters, which leads to a reduction in anxiety. However, the neurotransmitter GABA is an inhibitor (a natural one) of the fear response, and when certain drugs are taken that affect GABA, they actually lead to increased inhibition of the fear response. To make this clearer, think of endorphins—the body's natural painkillers. When you get hurt, endorphins are released in your brain to decrease the brain's ability to process pain signals. If it is not enough, we can take a pain medication that will have similar effects (as if we were to add more endorphins to our brain chemistry, or somehow make those endorphins stronger). GABA is similar to endorphins, but it works on the fear system, and certain drugs make it work even more.

We are still learning exactly how all of these chemicals work in the brain. This is partly because of the vast complexity of the brain and partly because we are limited in the types of studies that we can do with humans—we cannot actually go into the brain and observe it working. Just how dopamine, GABA, serotonin, and any other neurochemicals exactly work in the brain will be the subject of much further research, and it will most likely take decades before we can reach any firm conclusions.

What are SSRIs, and how do they help treat OCD?

An SSRI is a selective serotonin reuptake inhibitor (it affects the neurotransmitter serotonin). This means that the drug prevents the reuptake of serotonin back into the neuron that released it.

When a neuron releases serotonin into the synapse between itself and another neuron, the releasing neuron then vacuums all of the serotonin back up so that it does not have to constantly remake serotonin again and again. If neurons had to do this, our bodies would have to use a lot of energy just to synthesize more and more serotonin. So, the "vacuum" turns on, sucks the serotonin in the synapse back up, and holds it until it needs to be released again.

With an SSRI shutting off the vacuum, more serotonin stays float-ing around in the synapse, which means more chances for it to bounce onto the other neurons, creating more charges and therefore more chances for action potentials. As more action potentials occur, then there is more activity in that area of the brain, and the increased level of activity can have a positive effect on OCD symptoms. For some patients, OCD decreases as serotonin levels increase.

Are there side effects to SSRIs?

Side effects associated with SSRIs can include headaches, nausea, insomnia, agitation, and sexual problems, including an inability to orgasm for both men and women and impotence in men. Of all of the drugs that we review in this chapter, SSRIs appear to be the safest at this time for treating OCD in adults. However, there are some concerns currently about some SSRIs and a potential increase in suicidal thoughts in adolescents.

What are the names of some SSRIs that have been used to treat OCD?

Some SSRIs that have been used for OCD are as follows: fluoxetine (Prozac), fluvoxamine (Luvox,), bupropion (Wellbutrin), paroxo-tine (Paxil), citrilopram (Celexa), sertralin (Zoloft), and escitalo-pram Oxalate (Lexapro). The specific SSRIs that have been indicated for OCD by the FDA are Prozac, Luvox, Zoloft, and Paxil.

What are tricyclic antidepressants, and how do they help OCD?

Tricyclic antidepressants affect two neurotransmitters at the same time—serotonin and norepinephrine. Similar to the SSRIs, tricyclics prevent the reuptake of these neurotransmitters back into the neuron that released them, leaving more in the synapse and an increased chance for action potentials.

Are there side effects to tricyclics?

Sedation can be a common side effect of tricyclics, along with dry mouth, visual disturbances, constipation, weight gain, erectile dysfunction, restlessness, dizziness, and an increased potential for seizures if you have had a seizure or a head injury in the past.

What are the names of some tricyclics that have been used to treat OCD?

One of the most supported medications for OCD is the tricyclic clomipramine (Anafranil). It is one of the few drugs that have been approved specifically as a treatment for OCD instead of anxiety in general, and it has the most research support for any drug on the market related to the treatment of OCD. Other tricyclics that may be used for OCD are amitriptyline (Elavil), trazodone (Desyrel), and buspirone (Buspar).

What are MAO inhibitors (MAOIs)?

MAOIs (monoamine oxidase inhibitors) are a class of drugs that inhibit the effect of monoamine oxidase, a chemical that breaks down the monoamine neurotransmitters, such as serotonin, norepinephrine, and dopamine. These are called monoamine neurotransmitters because monoamines are a base chemical in all of these neurotransmitters (this is an incredibly simplified description of a monoamine, but enough to get the general idea).

When someone takes MAOIs, the breakdown of serotonin and norepinephrine is inhibited, therefore raising their levels in the neurons and synapses and having a positive effect on mood and anxiety.

What are the side effects of MAOIs?

There are significant side effects related to MAOIs, and they are therefore not prescribed very often for OCD. If individuals taking MAOIs eat foods containing tyramine, there can be a serious problem with hypertension (high blood pressure). Therefore, foods such as aged cheeses, chocolate, red wines, soy sauce, and processed meats must be avoided.

If these foods are eaten while taking MAOIs, levels of norepinephrine may rise to dangerous levels and blood pressure can skyrocket, even leading to internal hemorrhaging. Further, do not take MAOIs in combination with other drugs that affect serotonin, as it could lead to the development of serotonin syndrome, a life threatening overabundance of serotonin, which can cause difficulties in cardiovascular functioning, coordination, digestion, and the ability to concentrate.

Other side effects can include dry mouth, insomnia, weight gain, and impotence in men or inability to achieve orgasm for women. Although these side effects are potentially severe, for some individuals who have tried all of the other medications and have not had any success, MAOIs can have some positive effects. However, they are typically used as a last resort.

What are the names of some MAOIs that have been used to treat OCD?

Some MAOIs, such as phenelzine (Nardil), imipramine (Tofranil), and tranylcypromine (Parnate), are possible drug treatments that can be tried for OCD, but typically only as a last resort after the other classes of medications have been attempted first.

What are benzodiazepines?

Benzodiazepines (BDZs) are antianxiety medications that specifically affect the neurotransmitter GABA. GABA is an inhibitory neurotransmitter, meaning it has a sedating effect on the brain. BDZs interact with specific neurons where GABA binds to them, increasing the potency of GABA and leading it to have even more inhibitory effects on those neurons. BDZs can help people with OCD experience a decrease in activity in their midbrain, which can help calm individuals and decrease the effects of their obsessions and their desire to do compulsions.

What are the side effects of benzodiazepines?

The BDZs can have some side effects, such as sedation and some short-term memory loss, but a larger concern is that BDZs can be addictive. Therefore, it is very important to take them as prescribed and to not just stop taking them. Withdrawal from BDZs can be dangerous and difficult, even resulting in seizures or death. They should be slowly tapered off of, not abruptly stopped.

BDZs can also cause birth defects, so it is important for women taking BDZs to be on birth control or to practice other safe sexual practices to prevent pregnancy. Finally, do not take BDZs and drink alcohol at the same time. The depressant effects of alcohol and the inhibitory effects of BDZs can have a negative effect on motor activity and can make driving dangerous, not to mention having a significant depressant effect on the central nervous system that can potentially result in a shutdown of basic bodily functions, such as breathing.

What are the names of some benzodiazepines that have been used to treat OCD?

There are many different BDZs; some commonly prescribed for OCD are alprazolam (Xanax), lorazepam (Ativan), diazepam (Valium), and clonazepam (Klonopin).

What are neuroleptics?

Neuroleptics are drugs that are typically used to treat psychotic disorders, such as schizophrenia. Individuals with psychotic disorders have usually lost touch with reality, and they have difficulty distinguishing what is real from what is not. They may be suffering from hallucinations—a perceptual experience that only they can see, hear, smell, taste, or feel—or delusions, which are, according to the *DSM-IV-TR* (2000), "erroneous beliefs that usually involve a misinterpretation of perceptions or experiences." People with delusions may believe that they are being followed or that certain signs are directed only at them, such as believing a roadside ad for a dating service to be a coded message for their eyes only. There are times when someone with OCD has difficulty distinguishing what is real from what is not—the obsessions take on a delusional quality—and that may call for the prescription of these types of drugs. Neuroleptics affect the neurotransmitter dopamine, either blocking its release or affecting its ability to transmit messages to other neurons.

Are there side effects to neuroleptics?

The most serious possible side effects of neuroleptics are tremors and potentially a disorder called tardive dyskinesia, which manifests as abnormal mouth and tongue movements. Parkinsonism can also develop, which is Parkinson's disorder–like symptoms that can occur when a person is taking the medication but that typically decrease when the medication is stopped. There can be dry mouth, dizziness, blurred vision, or constipation as well. However, some of the newer neuroleptics, called atypical antipsychotics, have far fewer side effects than the first-generation neuroleptics did.

What are the names of some neuroleptics that have been used to treat OCD?

Several neuroleptics have been used for the treatment of OCD. Some of them include clozapine (Clozaril), risperidone (Risperidol), and olanzapine (Zyprexa).

What is D-cycloserine?

D-cycloserine is a drug originally developed for the treatment of tuberculosis. However, it was found to have an interesting side effect—it helps people learn things faster. Because of this, research is currently underway to see if D-cycloserine can assist individuals who are undergoing exposure therapy to actually learn from the exposures more quickly than individuals who are not taking D-cycloserine. Initial results look promising, and D-cycloserine may one day be a useful tool in assisting individuals undergoing exposure therapy to streamline their therapy process.

Can you treat OCD with medications alone?

Yes—there are people who only take medications for OCD and feel that their disorder is well controlled. However, the majority of people do not report that they have enough improvement with just medications (the typical improvement rate from medications alone is 30 percent) and also require some therapy to see significant change. If a person has been successfully treated for OCD in the past with medications, it is possible that medications alone may be enough to get her back to the level of functioning that she wishes to achieve. Also, research shows that individuals who take medication in combination with therapy have fewer relapses than individuals who take medication alone.

Once you start the medications, is it a lifelong commitment?

There is no definite answer for this question. Some people may be able to be on a medication for a period of time and then stop it and still see good results, whereas others may need to be on a medication for the rest of their lives.

One difficulty with medications can be something called state-dependent learning, wherein you learn how to handle a situation depending on the state that you are in. If you are taking medications and expose yourself to a certain stressful situation, then you may attribute your success to the medication and not to the fact that you chose to face the situation. If that is the case, then coming off the medication will change the state you are in, therefore leading to an increased chance of relapse into OCD when you face that situation again.

Therefore, when weaning off of medications, it is best to combine the process with some CBT and ERP so that the effects you start to lose from the medications are replaced by the skills you learn in therapy. By the time the medications are discontinued completely, the skills learned from therapy will be there to replace the former medication benefits.

What if I cannot afford the medications for my OCD?

There are plenty of programs available from pharmaceutical companies to assist people who are having difficulties paying for their medications, such as the Lilly Cares Program (www.lillycares.com;

800-545-6962). Other companies have similar services and will have up-to-date information on their websites.

Many insurance companies include a drug benefit as part of their plan, so often only a co-payment is necessary, and the ever-changing Medicare guidelines have provisions for medication costs as well. Also, many psychiatrists have sample packs of medications that they can give people to start them off on medications. They also occasionally get vouchers from pharmaceutical representatives, which can be used to help patients pay for medications. If you are having difficulties with paying for medications, your psychiatrist may be your best help because he or she will most likely have the information necessary for you to contact the drug companies to request specific assistance.

Is illegal drug use a problem for people with OCD?

Illegal drug use can be a problem for people with OCD if they turn to drugs as a way to try to drown out their obsessions. Some people turn to using illegal drugs as a way to try to handle their OCD instead of seeking therapy or legal medications. This can happen for several reasons—they may be too embarrassed to talk to anyone about their fears, or they may feel as if they are the only person with this problem, and therefore no one could help them anyway.

If you know someone who has OCD and is using illegal drugs as a way to try to handle his or her difficulties, please try to get that person to seek professional help. The first line of therapy will be to get the individual to break his or her addiction to illegal drugs, and then the correct medications can be prescribed, and/or a course of therapy can be begun, which can be far more successful in treating their OCD than the person's illegal drug use ever was or will be.

Chapter 9

LIVING WITH OCD

- Why does it seem that my OCD is easier to handle on some days than on other days?
- Don't we all have a bit of OCD from time to time?
- Am I a danger to others or myself?
- Will OCD decimate my social life?
- Is it possible to use your OCD to actually increase your abilities in certain areas and make you perform better at certain tasks?
- Why can't I be like everyone else and just do things normally?
- Does the Americans with Disabilities Act apply to OCD?
- How does OCD affect people on the job?
- What accommodations can be made on the job to assist a person with OCD?
- Can people with OCD inadvertently hurt other people because of the disorder?
- Does OCD spread? If I have a ritual of making sure the doors are locked, will it turn into making sure the windows are locked too?
- If you have suffered with OCD for over ten years, can you still recover?
- Why do people with OCD do things a certain number of times (such as turn the locks on the doors four times)?
- Can you die from OCD?
- I just had a baby and am having visions of drowning my child, so I make my husband do all of the bathing of the children. Will this assure my child's safety?
- I think that I have OCD—how do I tell my friends and family?
- I told my family that I have OCD, but they do not believe in psychology and think I am just going through a phase. How do I handle this?
- Why am I the only one in my family who has OCD?
- How can I be successful in college if I have OCD?
- How can I be a successful spouse if I have OCD?
- How can I be a successful parent if I have OCD?
- I am afraid that my child will be teased for having OCD—what can I do to prevent this from happening?

■ How can I be sure that my personal traits or quirks will not develop into OCD?

■ Why do I have obsessive thoughts about Jesus, Mary, God, and so on?

■ I believe that God will love me only if I am perfect. That is why I do rituals to undo any imperfections that I may have. How can I stop this?

■ How can I convince my eye doctor that I'm going blind and need him to check my eyes again, even though he has already given me an exam in the last thirty days?

■ Why do I confess to crimes I didn't commit, and how can I stop myself from doing it again?

■ I know it is not rational, but I think that I can get hepatitis from my garbage can—what can I do to overcome this?

Why does it seem that my OCD is easier to handle on some days than on other days?

This is an excellent question and one that baffles therapists and patients to this day. There are some days in which people report very little difficulty with an obsession or rarely perform a compulsion and other days in which the obsession is omnipresent or the compulsion is performed nearly nonstop.

Some possible explanations for this phenomenon follow:

- Other events or thoughts are distracting from the obsession that day.
- They recently gave in to the obsession or compulsion and exhausted themselves performing the ritual, which relieved them of it for a few days.
- General stress levels are known to have an impact on OCD behaviors, leading often to increased obsessions and compulsions.
- They may have missed a dose of medication, and the resulting change in medication levels had a negative effect on their OCD.

• They saw something on television or read a story about something that they fear, and it scared them enough that they went back to doing rituals.

These are just some possible reasons why people with OCD may see changes in their behavior. No one knows of an exact reason why it may happen, and it may be a combination of several of these or other reasons.

Don't we all have a bit of OCD from time to time?

No, we do not all have a bit of OCD from time to time. What all people have are their own unique traits, desires, and quirks. Most of the time, these quirks do not interfere in our lives or cause any significant distress, and therefore they are not classified as OCD. These personal traits can develop into OCD over time, but there is no guarantee that this will happen.

For example, consider that a man brushes his teeth in a certain order every evening—top front, top left, top right, bottom front, bottom left, bottom right. He may do this on a daily basis, and it is just a habit—one that he does not pay much attention to and that causes him no distress—so it does not meet the criteria for OCD. Further, if he were to not brush his teeth one night, he might think nothing of it. Yet, say one night while brushing his teeth, he is interrupted by a telephone call, and the caller tells him some bad news. He hangs up the phone and finishes brushing his teeth. The next night, as he is brushing his teeth, he may remember that he received a bad call while he was brushing. As he brushes, he may hope not to get another phone call and be very focused on the process of the brushing. Over time, as days and weeks pass, he may become increasingly focused on his brushing and hoping that he does not get a bad call.

The brushing and the potential for a bad call have become linked in his mind, so he begins to think that as long as he is not interrupted while brushing, and he does it in the correct order, everything will be fine. As time goes on, he may find that the brushing gets rougher, or the pattern is repeated again and again, just to be sure that his teeth are really clean, because they were not really clean when the original bad call came, and therefore, maybe unclean teeth are a sign of bad things to come. This may lead him to start brushing his teeth multiple times a day to try to prevent more and more bad things from happening.

As you can see, there are many ways that an obsession and compulsion can develop out of one small experience.

Am I a danger to others or myself?

This is a difficult question. People can inadvertently become a danger to themselves by performing certain rituals, such as washing their hands so many times that they scrub off layers of skin or scalding themselves in boiling hot water to remove germs. People with OCD can also inadvertently become a danger to others. For instance, the person who hits a bump in the road and thinks he or she hit someone may spend the next few minutes looking more in the rearview mirror than at the road ahead, therefore increasing his or her chance of hitting someone instead of decreasing it.

The bottom line is that OCD can contribute to your doing the very things you fear because of your lack of attention to your surroundings when you are ritualizing. It can also increase your chances of experiencing the very things that you fear because no one is ever able to perfectly avoid their obsessive thoughts, impulses, or images. Finally, OCD can increase the chances that you will inadvertently harm yourself because of the time and energy it requires. Obsessive thoughts and compulsive behaviors can interfere with your ability to perform in school or at work, potentially leading to poor perform-ance and to dropping out or getting fired.

Will OCD decimate my social life?

You can absolutely have a social life if you have OCD—having OCD does not mean that you have to shut yourself off from soci-ety. There are many people who have OCD and still go to work, attend social events, and perform the daily tasks required to main-tain a household. In fact, you may know people with OCD who have never told you that they have the disorder, and you may have never noticed.

A diagnosis of OCD does not have to impair your social function-ing. It may have some impact on your functioning, but it can range from not at all noticeable to very noticeable. If you are comfortable talking about your OCD with others, they may not care if you do your rituals around them. However you may choose to address your OCD with others, having the disorder does not mean that you are a social outcast.

Is it possible to use your OCD to actually increase your abilities in certain areas and make you perform better at certain tasks?

Some people with OCD believe that their OCD does help them in certain areas, and in the short run, this is possible. For example, the first few times you reread a paper for mistakes, you will probably find and correct some. However, in the long run, helpfulness will most likely not be the case—OCD obsessions tend to get worse over time, rituals tend to take longer to perform, and the number of occurrences increases. As your checking behavior gets worse, you may go from being satisfied with checking a paper twice to having to check it ten times just to be sure that everything is perfect, which is not a good use of your time.

Thinking that OCD is helpful to you is a slippery slope to tread on because the OCD will most likely just get worse over time, and you will feel more compelled to give in to it than to fight it if you think it's helping you. When you are at the point that you are giving in to your OCD, your performance does nothing but decrease.

Why can't I be like everyone else and just do things normally?

You can be like everyone else and do things normally; you may just need some therapy in order to make that happen. If you believe that you can't do things normally, you won't. However, if you understand that it is your OCD that is interfering with your ability to do things in a socially acceptable way, then you are a step ahead of people who have given up hope.

Excellent therapies are available for OCD and can help you get back to the life that you led before the OCD became a burden. It is very possible to get back to that level of functioning—you just need to believe that you can get there, and you need to work hard at overcoming your OCD. There is no reason that you cannot return to that level of functioning if you follow through with what your therapist asks you to do.

Does the Americans with Disabilities Act apply to OCD?

Although the Americans with Disabilities Act does not specifically mention OCD, it does apply to individuals with the disorder. That being said, it is a law and therefore can be interpreted in many ways. The legal statute states, "The ADA does not list any specific disabilities at all. Rather, it provides a loose definition of disability, which allows the attorneys and courts to make the determination on a case-by-case basis." Disability is defined as "a physical or mental impairment that substantially limits a major life activity." This is broken into a two-part test:

1. Is the person impaired?
2. Does the impairment substantially limit a major life activity?

Although OCD might easily meet the criterion in number 1, number 2 is subject to interpretation by lawyers, employers, and the court system. The key words are "substantially" and "major." If it's not clearly a major life activity, or the limitations do not appear to be substantial, you're probably not going to be covered. Major life activities, according to the Equal Employment Opportunity Commission (EEOC), include functions such as caring for oneself, performing manual tasks, walking, seeing, hearing, speaking, breathing, learning, and working. Substantial limitation, according to the EEOC, is defined as "significantly restricted in the ability to perform either a class of jobs or a broad range of jobs in various classes as compared to the average person having comparable training, skills and abilities." The inability to perform a single, particular job does not constitute a substantial limitation in the major life activity of working.

As far as employment discrimination goes, a person must be qualified to perform the job duties in order to be protected by ADA. This basically means that a person must satisfy the employer's job requirements (such as education, experience, skill set, licenses, and so on) and must be able to perform the essential job functions with or without reasonable accommodations. Reasonable accommodations can also be subject to interpretation by lawyers, employers, and the courts. Some potential accommodations for anxiety disorders and OCD are flexible scheduling, extra leave, extra time to learn new tasks or information, added partitions to help concentration, reduction of distractions (e.g., co-workers' radios), or telecommuting.

A particular section of the EEOC's website, http://www. eeoc.gov/policy/docs/902cm.html, is a great resource for information and interpretation of the Americans with Disabilities Act. It would be best to consult a lawyer who specializes in disability cases to see just how the ADA may apply to your specific case of OCD.

How does OCD affect people on the job?

OCD can have many negative impacts on job performance. Some individuals may spend increasing amounts of time in the bathroom washing their hands to deal with germ fears. Others may spend large amounts of time cleaning their desks or straightening things instead of actually doing their work. Or when they are doing their work, people with OCD may try to do it so perfectly that they are unable to do things in a timely manner—they may keep erasing things that they think aren't quite right, keep retyping e-mails, or even have the inability to start a project because they have to have the "perfect" first move.

It is also possible for people with OCD to be so worried about things at home—the coffee pot or stove being left on, the doors being unlocked, and so on—that they'll leave work, maybe repeatedly, to go check on things. They could also be habitually late because they are so caught up in their rituals at home in the morning.

OCD can also make people hesitate. If they are constantly questioning themselves or seeking safety, they may put themselves or others in danger inadvertently. If, for example, you are a delivery person, and you have a ritual where you stand still and hold your breath for twenty seconds every time you hear someone swear, this could lead to great difficulties if, while crossing the street, someone in front of you swears and you end up doing your ritual in the middle of an intersection. You could get hit by a car or cause a traffic jam.

However OCD is experienced on the job, it can surely interfere with a person's ability to function at maximum potential. It's best to seek some form of therapy to challenge the OCD and combat its effects on job performance.

What accommodations can be made on the job to assist a person with OCD?

First, review the Americans with Disabilities Act (ADA) (see question "Does the Americans with Disabilities Act apply to OCD?" on page 182) and become familiar with its provisions—that may be the best way to know your exact rights as a worker. Further, consulting a lawyer who specializes in the ADA may be a good idea. Such a lawyer may be able to help you with any work-related questions you may have. If there is someone you trust in your human resources office, you may want to talk with that person about your OCD so that he or she is aware that you may require some special accommodations.

It may be best to look for a job that is not too stressful, especially if you have not gotten treatment for your OCD. Stress can make OCD symptoms worse, so you probably want to avoid it as much as possible until you start to get treatment and can learn to handle increasing levels of stress. But, you're in danger of even losing a low-stress job if it incites your OCD symptoms to the point where the symptoms interfere in your work.

If you are already receiving treatment for your OCD, then be sure to discuss your work life with your therapist because he or she may be able to give you advice about how best to handle your OCD in the workplace. Or if you can identify specific obsessions you have or compulsions you perform at work, then you and your therapist can practice specific exposures to challenge them. If you are taking medications, be sure to keep taking them as prescribed, and if you identify any side effects, tell your doctor right away so that he or she may work with you on adjusting the medications as necessary. Further, if you are in need of a therapist, your employee assistance program may be able to help you locate one. This is often a free service that many companies provide to their employees.

Finally, feel free to take a personal day every few months if you have them available. They are there for a reason—so that people can take a break now and then. If you feel stress building up and are afraid you may start to perform rituals again, it is OK to take a break and allow yourself the chance to relax.

Can people with OCD inadvertently hurt other people because of the disorder?

People with OCD do not want to purposely hurt anyone—of course, some do have obsessions about hurting others, but that does not mean that they want to hurt anyone. In fact, it is most often just the opposite; they want to do all that they can to be sure that they bring no harm to anyone. However, there are times that the OCD behavior becomes so overwhelming that they do something they know to be logically wrong.

For example, families of an individual with OCD can experience great emotional burdens. They may get into arguments about rituals or may become very sad at watching their loved one do things that do not seem at all logical. Also, by doing their rituals, individuals with OCD may inadvertently harm someone. If a person with OCD is afraid of germs and is watching a child, that person may refuse to change a diaper or help a child clean him- or herself, which may lead to a rash or infection. This chance of accidentally harming another person is yet another compelling reason to seek treatment for OCD.

Does OCD spread? If I have a ritual of making sure the doors are locked, will it turn into making sure the windows are locked too?

Not necessarily, but it is possible; and it's likely if the OCD goes untreated. The course of OCD is not 100 percent predictable, so it is impossible to say for sure whether OCD rituals will morph into other areas. If OCD were to spread, it would most likely be in the same theme though, such as the checking mentioned in the question. Checking a door and checking a window can be easily related to each other, whereas checking a door and then hoarding all of your newspapers are not related to each other. This type of migration would be less likely to occur.

If you have suffered with OCD for over ten years, can you still recover?

Absolutely. Be it ten months, ten years, or thirty years, individuals with OCD can always benefit from treatment and get better. As long as they are willing to challenge themselves and to listen to the advice of their treatment providers (such as to do exposures and to take their medications as prescribed), there is no reason that they cannot be successfully treated.

The biggest deterrent to getting better would be to believe that it is too late for therapy to be of any assistance. Without therapy it may be very difficult for people to get better on their own, especially if they have had OCD for so long. That is why it is important for people to find specialized treatment providers who will be able to assist in their recovery.

Why do people with OCD do things a certain number of times (such as turn the locks on the doors four times)?

People with OCD stick with a number for their rituals because that number feels right or is comfortable for them. They may think certain numbers, or multiples of that number, are safe, and therefore they only do things that number of times. Why that specific number is chosen may be random (they may have done a ritual a certain number of times one day and later remembered that it felt good, so they stuck with it), or there may be a meaning attached to it (because there are that many members in their family, they need to do it that many times to be sure that all of the family members are safe).

Not all people with OCD do things a certain number of times— some just keep doing rituals until they feel as if they were done just right or perfectly. Others just have to do them for a set number of times, and some need to do both—they have to do the rituals for a certain number of times perfectly before they can stop the ritual. If even one ritual is done wrong, even if it is the last in the series, they will often start all over again, continuing until the series is completed perfectly before they will go on to do the next ritual or task in their day.

Can you die from OCD?

OCD will not kill you. However, it is possible to die as a result of doing a ritual. For example, if every time you hit a bump while driving you look in the rearview mirror to see if you hit someone, it's possible that your distraction in looking for a body could lead to your getting into an accident. If you are a hoarder, and your house if full of papers and other items, and there is a fire, it may be almost impossible for you to get out because of the amount of fuel for the fire and the likely rapidity with which the fire will spread. Or if you are a washer, you could possibly do so much damage to your skin that you get some serious infections that could make their way into your bloodstream and lead to your death. While these are all rare occurrences, they are possible, and could be the result of doing rituals.

I just had a baby and am having visions of drowning my child, so I make my husband do all of the bathing of the children. Will this assure my child's safety?

No, this will not assure your child's safety. Your child is already safe with you. Now, that may sound scary, especially in light of recent stories in the news of women drowning their children, but recognize that the media often publicizes the most gory and shocking stories it can find (as the saying goes, "if it bleeds, it leads"). Although these cases do happen now and then, they are so rare that the chances of them happening to you and your child are amazingly slim. You have a better chance of dying in a car accident while driving your child to the doctor than you do of drowning your child. Further, these women meet criteria for diagnoses other than OCD—they often talk about hearing voices telling them to sacrifice their children, which is more akin to the diagnosis of major depressive disorder with psychotic features than it is to OCD.

That being said, the more that you ignore bathing your child, the more likely you will fear it, convincing yourself that the only reason your child is safe is because your husband does the bathing. If you really want to get help with this, it may be best to talk to a therapist about your fears. A therapist can help normalize your concerns (many women, especially new mothers, have thoughts about harming their children—it is not uncommon at all) and start you on an exposure therapy protocol for bathing your child. Your therapist may have you do some bathing with a sponge first, working up to a small bucket of water, and then moving to the sink or the bathtub. They may also have your husband stay with you at first for initial reassurance, having him slowly decrease the amount of time he is supervising you with your baby. Finally, you will be able to be alone with your child around water and recognize that just because you have thoughts about harming your child does not mean that you actually will harm your child.

A recent area of research for OCD is postpartum OCD. Remember, it was mentioned earlier that having a child can be a stressor that can be an OCD trigger. This new area of study will hopefully lead to some fruitful ideas for treatment of people who find themselves with OCD symptoms after the birth of a child.

I think that I have OCD—how do I tell my friends and family?

If you had cancer, what would you tell your friends and family? Probably that you had cancer. Why is telling them you have OCD any different? If OCD is a serious problem in your life, then it will be helpful for you to have the support of people who love and care for you. Talk to them about your fears, and let them know how they can help you because most of them will offer to anyway. Even if it is just having them check in on you, let others know what they can do to help.

There is an unfortunate stigma about mental illness—even though there are actually more people with anxiety than there are with cancer, we still think we need to hide the anxiety. The more you are open about your difficulties with the people you trust, the more you will influence them to be open about mental disorders. That influence will grow exponentially over time, and hopefully there will be a day when people will not be ashamed to say they have a problem, no matter what it is.

I told my family that I have OCD, but they do not believe in psychology and think I am just going through a phase. How do I handle this?

Though others in your life may not be very supportive at this time, it does not mean that you have to let it negatively impact you: you can still seek treatment on your own and start to work on your OCD. Although it may be easier to have the support of people in your family, you may be able to win them over by showing them that you can change your behavior with the help of a therapist or medication. They may then start to see that there is some benefit to mental health therapy and psychology.

If your family is not supportive, maybe there are some friends who could be or a support group that you could join to meet others who have OCD. There are many people besides your family on whom you can rely at this time—seek them out. Either way, find someone who will help give you the strength you need to get help.

Why am I the only one in my family who has OCD?

There are many possible reasons for that. You may be the only person in your family with a genetic marker for OCD. Because of this, you had a higher probability of developing it. Or you were the only person to get PANDAS in your family, and therefore your OCD was a result of a strep infection. It is possible that you are the only person in your family who had a reaction to an intrusive thought that led to obsessive thinking or the desire to do a ritual. When you did the ritual, it felt relieving, leading to the chance of that happening again in the future. Whatever the reason, it does not say anything bad about you as a person—it just means that you have a difficulty, and you need to get help for it.

How can I be successful in college if I have OCD?

This may depend on what your OCD focuses on. If it is related to your schoolwork, you may have difficulty accomplishing work in your classes. For example, if you try to read every source available on a topic to be sure that your paper does not sound as if you are inadvertently plagiarizing someone else's work, you may spend so much time reading other works that you do not actually complete your paper. Or, you may fear turning it in because you worry that the professor will think that you stole other writers' work. Further, if you are obsessive about finding all of the sources for a topic or making sure your work is perfect before you turn it in, you will probably only get one or two papers turned in all semester. That could have an extremely negative impact on your grades.

However, OCD may also have a significant impact on schooling even if it is not related to school work, such as in the case of the following obsession: "Did I turn off my curling iron? What if I did not and the house is on fire?" It is easy to see how this could interfere with your ability to stay focused in class. You may even leave class just to go home and be sure it is off, or try to call someone to have that person check on the house for you. Some individuals are able to suppress their rituals while they are at school, but once they get home, the rituals may start and last hours. This could interfere with the ability to complete homework or projects in a timely fashion.

You can take several steps to help ensure success in school. First, most colleges or universities have a counseling center. Check to see if any therapists there are specialists in OCD. Be sure you check to see if they use CBT and ERP, because many college counseling centers, unfortunately, do not have many people on staff who do this type of therapy. If there is no one at the center, then there are probably therapists in the surrounding area of the university who have some training in OCD. Second, if you are on medications, be sure to stay in contact with your psychiatrist, let him or her know how things are going throughout the semester, and schedule periodic visits with the psychiatrist during breaks or holidays for medication checks. Do the same if you have been seeing a therapist at home. Third, you may want to tell your professors about your OCD so that they are aware that there may be occasions when you will need some extra time to get things completed. Many professors are willing to work with their students to help them be successful in their classes. If you find you are having difficulties with some of your professors, you can always turn to the university ombudsman (a person designated to help with any complaints or concerns) or with the student affairs office, which may have someone who specializes in disability issues.

Finally, you may also need to be open about your OCD with your college roommates so that they are aware of why you do certain things that may seem odd. Let them know how best to respond to your rituals, reassurance-seeking, or avoidance of certain things so that they will not just think you are "weird" or spread rumors about you throughout the dorm.

How can I be a successful spouse if I have OCD?

There is a book by Karen Landsman, Kathleen Rupertus, and Cherry Pedrick called *Loving Someone with* OCD (2005) that addresses this question in great detail. The book discusses many topics, from intimacy to creating contracts about decreasing reassurance-seeking. It contains many different charts and exercises for spouses to do together, such as creating a log of accommodating behaviors to decrease (behaviors that your spouse may do to assist you with your OCD, such as helping you with your rituals or giving you reassurance when you seek it), setting up a family contract about how you and your spouse will handle the OCD together, and even how you can, as a couple, find a therapist or a support group.

The goal of a marriage is to be able to work together. Although having OCD may make this more difficult, it is not impossible. It takes effort, but couples can devise a mutually beneficial plan that will address their emotional, physical, and mental health needs.

How can I be a successful parent if I have OCD?

The first thing to realize is that the OCD is your OCD and not your children's. Therefore, if they do not perform up to what your obsessions tell you are necessary standards, or they clean in a way that you find unacceptable (according to your OCD), it is not fair for you to be angry at them or to take out your frustrations on them.

Being a successful parent is difficult even without OCD, and there are no guarantees, even if you have the best mental health in the world, that your children will turn out to be "angels." That said, you can be a successful parent if you have OCD by doing something to take care of yourself, and that means going to therapy or staying on a prescribed dosage of medication. Be sure that you follow through with the recommendations of your therapist and that you talk to the therapist if you feel that your OCD is having an impact on your family. If you want your OCD to have as little impact as possible on your children, then you need to do whatever it takes to keep yourself healthy.

Also, some family therapy may also be beneficial. Your therapist can explain to your family what OCD is and how it affects you, therefore giving them some helpful information about the disorder, in addition to tips that they can use to assist you in your therapy.

I am afraid that my child will be teased for having OCD—what can I do to prevent this from happening?

First, get your child into therapy as soon as you possibly can so that your child can begin to decrease his or her OCD behaviors right away. Second, it would be helpful to sit down with a counselor at the child's school to let him or her know about your child's OCD and in what areas your child has difficulties. Schools can often make certain accommodations for children to assist them with their disorders. For example, it may be best to excuse a child from art class if the child has obsessive fears of getting stains on his or her clothing. Once therapy has started to work on this area, then the child can slowly be reintegrated into art class.

Some parents find it helpful to talk to the parents of their children's friends to let them know about the OCD and what things may set off an obsession or a ritual. This way the other parents won't be alarmed if the child starts to act in a "strange" manner. Finally, you and your child can explain to his or her friends what OCD is and why your child acts certain ways at times. Often, these friends will accept this and even stick up for the child if other kids start to tease him or her.

How can I be sure that my personal traits or quirks will not develop into OCD?

There is little danger of your personal traits or quirks developing into OCD if you are an adult and have not already been diagnosed or have not found obsessions and compulsions to be affecting your daily life. Everyone has his or her own unique traits and specific ways of doing things—it is what makes us human. If we all did things the same way, the world would be a pretty boring place.

The difficulty arises if you are unable to do behaviors in a way that is different from how you normally like to do them. If that brings about significant distress, an OCD diagnosis may be warranted. However, if you could change your behavior pattern to accommodate an interruption, such as not being able to vacuum the entire house the way that you like because guests have arrived early, then your traits have little chance of developing into OCD. If, however, you would make your guests wait outside until you finished vacuuming, or you would spend the entire time at your party worrying about what people were thinking about you because you had not yet vacuumed, then it is possible that OCD is a difficulty for you.

Why do I have obsessive thoughts about Jesus, Mary, God, and so on?

This is a fairly common OCD obsession, often complete with compulsions. Let's say that you believe Jesus, Mary, and God view you as a sinner and are waiting to strike you down with lightning; therefore, every time there's a storm, you have to hide in a closet and count to seven three times in order to be safe. (The numbers people use are often typical numbers for a religious obsession—the number seven is often seen as lucky in our culture, and the number three is often used because of the trinity in the Christian religion.) However, there is a flaw in this logic—if God is really all-powerful, then it does not matter what you count to or where you hide because that lightning is going to find you.

Most likely, you are not as afraid of what a higher power thinks of you as you are of what you think of yourself. The more negative you are to yourself, the more difficult it will be for you to stop doing the rituals—you will rely on them for relief from the obsessive thoughts. You have to work on first accepting yourself, negative or sinful thoughts and all, and then recognize that you are probably not much different from anyone else you know, except for the fact that you treat yourself much more harshly, and then you use the threat of hellfire and damnation as a way to try to motivate yourself to be better. This will most likely lead to only feeling worse, and the cycle of rituals will just continue.

I believe that God will love me only if I am perfect. That is why I do rituals to undo any imperfections that I may have. How can I stop this?

One way would be to consider this: You probably believe that God is perfect and that only God is perfect. Therefore, you are basically telling yourself that in order to be accepted by God, you must actually be God—because if God only accepts perfection, then the only person God loves is . . . God.

You have set yourself up to fail automatically by setting a goal that is unattainable—perfection. Because you cannot be perfect—no one can—you think you are unacceptable. Your belief in your unacceptability is the real source of the problem. Until you believe that you are acceptable as you are, with all of your flaws and imperfections, you are just going to beat yourself up for not being perfect, which will mean beating yourself up for the rest of your life. And it is rather doubtful that your religion really wants you to spend the rest of your life condemning yourself when you could be influencing others by your example of bettering yourself. To stop this obsession, seek help from a professional.

How can I convince my eye doctor that I'm going blind and need him to check my eyes again, even though he has already given me an exam in the last thirty days?

Just because you think you will go blind does not actually mean that you will go blind. In a similar vein, if you look at the moon tonight and think that it will explode in the next five seconds—it probably won't.

It is a good thing that your doctor will not give you another exam. For practical purposes, your insurance probably covers only one exam per year, so your eye doctor would not be able to do it anyway unless you were going to pay out of pocket. Your doctor is also probably aware that some people have anxiety concerns about their health, and OCD can surely be focused on health. OCD fears can lead a person to get checked out by many different doctors, to want numerous tests for disorders or diseases that are extremely rare, or to spend hours on the Internet researching signs and symptoms. Some therapists even ban their patients from using the Internet for a period of time during treatment so that they will not try to look up more disease information.

So it is not a good idea to try to convince your doctor to give you another exam because the relief that you will feel from that exam will be only temporary, until you obsess about your next symptom and want another exam to confirm that you are free from any disease. It would be better to seek treatment about your health obsessions so that you can learn how to handle your fears instead of needing constant reassurance from medical professionals.

Why do I confess to crimes I didn't commit, and how can I stop myself from doing it again?

This is actually a more common OCD experience than people would think: You saw a story on the news about a hit-and-run accident in the town next to yours. You called the police to tell them you might have done it, and they came to your house and questioned you. When you told them you were not sure if you had driven that day, and then they saw that your car did not match the description given by witnesses, they yelled at you and threatened to take you to jail for making a false complaint. Why did you make that call, and how can you stop yourself from doing it again?

Many times, people with OCD who have a fear of harming people will drive around a block several times if they hit a bump as a way to be sure that they have not hit anyone. They will often drive very slowly looking for the body, or they will drive over the bump again and again to see if they hear the same sound as they did the first time. If it was a different sound, then they will search even harder for the body, thinking that they really did hit someone.

Individuals with this fear may perform several different behaviors. Some will listen to the news intently every day to try to find out if they may have hit someone, whereas others may try to avoid the news as much as possible so that they do not have to deal with the possibility that they may have harmed someone. And some will go so far as to call the police to turn themselves in for something that they did not do, but that they fear they might have done, despite all evidence to the contrary.

This type of OCD may be fueled by guilt. Of course, their OCD will ensure that these people make all attempts, reasonable and unreasonable, to avoid harming someone, but the OCD can also take the form of demanding punishment for possibly harming someone. So, OCD may influence people to rarely drive or to do so only when it is absolutely necessary, such as going to work. But if something happens while they are driving—even a small thing, such as hitting a bump or getting a speeding ticket—then the OCD may lead to many guilt-laden thoughts that will torment them until they are punished for their transgressions through a ritual, such as confessing to a crime they couldn't have committed.

In order to not make the call to the police again in the future, you will need to realize a few things. First, the chance of actually hitting a person with your car is very low. Second, the chance that you will hit someone and not know you did is even smaller. Third, the chance that you would hit someone and drive away is even less. Therefore, it is amazingly unlikely that you will be the cause of harm to a pedestrian with your car.

However, because your OCD has picked this as the thing to fear the most, the odds really do not matter. Therefore, you need to purposely expose yourself to driving.

You can work with a therapist who will drive with you and start driving in wide-open spaces. You can drive, hit potholes, and get used to not checking in your mirrors for bodies (many therapists will have you turn your mirrors to face the ground so that you cannot use them). Then a therapist can have you drive by him or her slowly, to see what it is like to pass by someone. The therapist might even throw things at your car, such as a pillow, so that you can see that you would be able to tell if something were to bounce off of your vehicle. Finally, you can move up to driving through regular streets and eventually next to parks or other places where there are a lot of people. This slow exposure will probably be very helpful in getting you back out driving again.

I know it is not rational, but I think that I can get hepatitis from my garbage can—what can I do to overcome this?

Yes, this is an irrational thought, but there are things you can do to challenge it. First, look at this fear from a rational perspective: How many people do you know who have contracted hepatitis? Second, how many people have contracted any disease from a garbage can? Third, how many people have contracted hepatitis from a garbage can? Fourth, can you find a research article about the dangers of people contracting hepatitis from garbage cans? Fifth, why are you so afraid of hepatitis?

Let's look at each of these questions and how they may be used in therapy. The first question is a question of probability—most of us do not know many, if any, people who have contracted hepatitis. And, for those that have been infected, many have recovered and have developed antibodies to fight future infections. That is not to say it is not a serious condition—it is—but this is a question of probability. The second question looks at the source of the contamination to see how realistic the scenario is. Garbage cans may be dirty, but are not seen as huge sources of contamination in everyday life, or we would have seen major warnings on the news to never touch garbage cans. Also, trash collectors would be dying by the dozens. The third question melds the first two together. If you do not know many people who have hepatitis, then chances are there are not many people with hepatitis using your garbage can. And, since the potential for getting an illness from a personal garbage can is low, then it stands to reason that the chance of getting hepatitis from your own garbage can is low. In fact, in order to get infected with hepatitis from your own garbage can, you would probably already have to be infected with hepatitis—otherwise, how could you really get it?

The fourth question gets to the realism of the fear—are there warnings out there to not touch your own garbage cans? The answer is no. If our own garbage cans were a source of hepatitis and touching them exposed us to hepatitis, then everyone who has ever taken out their own trash, much less anyone else's, would have to be infected with hepatitis. Looking on the Centers for Disease Control website, there are no warnings about hepatitis outbreaks linked to garbage cans (www.cdc.gov).

The fifth question gets to the source of the fear—what is it about hepatitis that is so fear-inducing? You may know someone with it and may have seen that it was a very difficult experience for that person. Or you may see it as a disgusting disease and want to prevent it at all costs. Or maybe you think that people who contract it are disgusting, and you do not want to become what you think is so gross. No matter what the reason, your thinking something about hepatitis does not mean that it is true. People who get hepatitis did not want to get it. Whereas some contract it because of unsafe behaviors, others get it even though they perform all of the proper safety behaviors. Some people do die of hepatitis, but many also recover and develop antibodies to it. There are two sides to look at when discussing this disease.

The best way to avoid hepatitis is to wash your hands before you prepare food and after going to the bathroom, to not use intravenous drugs, and to practice safe sex. These precautions will eliminate most of the risks of hepatitis contamination. Not touching your garbage can will just lead to garbage piling up and the unfortunate effects of that, such as the smell of rotting food, fruit flies, and vermin.

Chapter 10

TALKING ABOUT OCD WITH OTHERS

- I keep telling my friend to stop her rituals, but she won't. Why can't she just stop?
- Help me to understand how my husband can believe that his breathing a certain way will somehow prevent something bad from happening to me.
- I am embarrassed to have people come to my home because it is literally filled with stuff that my father hoards. What can I do to help him start getting rid of it?
- What is the best way to approach someone whom you think has OCD to let that person know that he or she may need treatment?
- What do you do if a person with OCD refuses help?
- How should I react to someone with OCD?
- What are some things that family members can do for people with OCD in their family?
- Why does my friend with OCD always say that this will be the last time she does a ritual, when I know that this is not true?
- What if my partner will not leave the house because he is doing a ritual and we need to be somewhere?

I keep telling my friend to stop her rituals, but she won't. Why can't she just stop?

It is as easy for her to just stop her rituals as it would be for you to just stop yourself from jumping out of the way of a car that is coming toward you at 50 miles per hour. When she is doing a ritual, it is a fear response to an obsessive thought, impulse, or image. So she may think that she needs to straighten out everything in her house and put all items at 90 degree angles on all tables because of a fear that if she did not, something horrible would happen to her family. How those items and her family's safety are related is not as important as her belief that she has to do her rituals or she will be responsible for some horrible fate befalling her family. Therefore, stopping the ritual, to her, would ensure that something bad would happen to her family, and she is not willing to take that risk. That is why she cannot just stop doing the ritual—what seems annoying and illogical to you seems absolutely necessary to her.

Help me to understand how my husband can believe that his breathing a certain way will somehow prevent something bad from happening to me.

The easy part of this answer is that the breathing a certain way is a compulsive behavior that he performs to try to undo an obsessive thought or image about you being harmed. The more difficult part of the answer involves trying to help you understand why he does this. (To get an idea of what a breathing ritual can look like if you've never seen one, try to watch the MTV show *True Life: I Have OCD* (2005). On that show is a male who does a lot of breathing rituals, in addition to many other compulsive behaviors.)

Let's think about some possible reasons for the breathing ritual. It is possible that your husband once had an intrusive thought about you being harmed as he was yawning. That feeling of not breathing when yawning could have been paired with a thought of you being harmed and it caused him more anxiety than the thought alone would have. Now he wants to be sure that he breathes a certain way to be sure that no harm will come to you, as well as to prevent himself from experiencing the anxiety associated with not breathing.

Or maybe one day he saw you almost get hit by a car, and as you were about to get harmed, he took a deep breath (as would be common), and just as he did that, the car swerved. He may have paired in his head the breathing and the car swerving, so he feels that he needs to continue to breathe that way to keep you safe, even if he's combating only a thought about something bad happening to you.

Whatever the reason for them, the breathing rituals will probably seem very strange to you, and in a way that is good because it means you can help your husband see the irrationality of the thought. As strange as it sounds, his motivation really is to keep you safe—but as noble as his intentions may be, his compulsions are also extremely unnecessary, given that his breathing and your safety obviously have nothing to do with each other. And this is exactly what he will have to learn through therapy. You will probably not be able to just convince him to stop. Find a therapist who can assist both of you with this; it may be necessary to include you in the therapy so that your husband can see firsthand that not doing his rituals does not lead to any harm befalling you.

I am embarrassed to have people come to my home because it is literally filled with stuff that my father hoards. What can I do to help him start getting rid of it?

For his change to be truly successful, your father will have to want to discard some of the items that he has hoarded. If he does not want to do this, it will be difficult for him to change.

There are several ways to approach this situation. First, you could have a family meeting, where you and everyone else in your family sit down with your father and tell him how all of the stuff in the house is having a negative impact on you and how you are embarrassed to have people come over. Do not do this in an accusatory manner, but just be frank and let him know how you feel about the situation.

If he is willing to get some help, let him know that you will help in any way you can and that you know this will be difficult for him. If he is not willing to get help, then there are other options—however, just throwing out all of the stuff when he is not around is probably not a good idea. That would most likely make him very angry and would also probably make the hoarding worse because there is a good chance that he would seek out more items to fill the void that you created by purging everything he already had.

One option that you have is to tell him that if he is not going to get help, the rest of the family will be moving into an apartment. Many families have done this in the past, some for sanitary and health reasons and others because they just could not stand living in such conditions anymore. You and the rest of your family can decide what rules to have at the apartment, what comes in and what gets thrown out. If your father chooses to visit, you can set it up so that he is not allowed to bring anything into the apartment other than one change of clothing and toiletries. Otherwise, he must keep the hoarding to the home. Although this may not be convenient, it is what some families have had to do.

Unfortunately, you cannot make your father change his behavior. You can, however, let him know how his behavior has impacted you and show him that you are willing to either help him or do something to place yourself in an environment where you will feel safe and comfortable.

What is the best way to approach someone whom you think has OCD to let that person know that he or she may need treatment?

There are several ways you may go about suggesting treatment to people whom you believe have OCD. The most direct approach is to just tell them that you have seen them performing some behaviors that appear to be rituals. Let them know that you have read about OCD, that you think they may be exhibiting some symptoms, and that you're willing to assist them in getting some help. Now, they may tell you that there is nothing wrong and that they have stopped doing whatever it is that you saw them doing. However, just let them know that you have noticed some things and they can come to you if they decide to pursue help.

You could also give them this book, telling them some of the behaviors they exhibit seem like something you saw in a movie or on a TV show, so you got this book to see if what they were doing was similar, and it looks as if it is. If you are not comfortable talking face to face, you could write them a letter or an email and tell them you are concerned about them. You could even send them links to some of the websites that are cited in this book.

Finally, if they do decide to go to talk to a therapist, you could offer to go with them. Even if they do not want you to talk to the therapist, you could at least give them some moral support by driving to the appointment with them and talking to them afterward to be sure that they felt comfortable with everything.

Just keep in mind that the best time to talk to someone would be as soon as you think that the person has OCD. The sooner a person starts to work on his or her OCD, the fewer effects he or she will have from it. Also, it will help to prevent the OCD from getting worse, therefore making the therapy potentially quicker.

What do you do if a person with OCD refuses help?

This is a difficult question because you will have to decide how you want to treat the person with OCD from today forward. If the person does not want any help, and the person's OCD does not interfere very much with his or her life or your life, then there is probably not much that you can do. However, if the OCD is interfering significantly, you do have some options.

First, let the person know that you are going to stop being a part of his or her rituals. If this person asks you to check things for him or her or asks for you to provide reassurance, tell the person that you are going to stop doing this because it's making his or her OCD worse instead of better, and your participation in his or her rituals is giving them the message that you also feel as if the ritual is important when, actually, you do not. Second, slowly stop making accommodations for the person's rituals. For example, if your child is always late for school due to performing certain morning rituals, and you call them in with an excused absence every morning, consider not calling them in and therefore having them face the consequences of being late for school. Third, let the person know that if he or she is not going to seek help, you are going to talk to someone about it. A therapist can sit down with you and talk to you about your specific situation and discuss what options may be best for you to help you stop accommodating the person with OCD in your life. Fourth, there may be support groups in your area for family members of OCD sufferers that you can join. The other members may be able to give you tips on living with a person with OCD who does not want help, or they may have some good ways to help convince the OCD sufferer to get help.

Finally, stick with your plan. As hard as it may be, and as much as the person may plead with you to help him or her, keep in mind that every time you accommodate one of his or her rituals, you are send-ing a message that the OCD is correct and that it needs to be accom-modated. This is simply not true. Let your loved one know that you are supporting him or her, but that you are not supporting the OCD, and when he or she is ready to challenge the OCD, you will be happy to assist in any way that you can.

How should I react to someone with OCD?

First, you are most likely already interacting with someone with OCD in your daily life without even being aware of it. There are so many people with OCD that it would be surprising if you did not know someone with the disorder. This person may be able to control his or her OCD enough at work or in social situations that you don't even notice it, or maybe it's manifested through mostly obsessions and mental rituals, so you never actually see the person performing any overt behavioral rituals.

If you do meet someone with OCD, and it's either apparent or the person tells you he or she has it, the best thing to do would be to treat the person, hopefully, like you would treat everyone else— with respect and compassion. People with OCD did not ask to have the disorder and desperately want to be rid of it, but they are facing fears that are very real to them, so they need support to get through their difficulties. That said, do not give a lot of reassurance to people with OCD. It may seem like a compassionate thing to do, but people with OCD are looking for reassurance, and you may unwittingly play right into their desire to attain immediate relief and feelings of safety. It is fine to encourage them to follow through on their therapy and challenge their fears, but it is a slippery slope when you give them reassurance, which will actually help to main-tain their OCD.

What are some things that family members can do for people with OCD in their family?

Family members can do several things to support the person or people with OCD in their family. First, they can become involved in the therapy. Having family members encourage the people with OCD to keep up their exposure therapy or take their medication can help them to challenge their OCD and not give in to it. Family members can also offer encouragement to people with OCD while they are doing their exposures. Family members can help move therapy along, because they may be able to tell the therapist what OCD behaviors they see being performed that the people with OCD may not even notice or may be too embarrassed to discuss. This can help therapists to be sure that they are designing exposures to fit all of the difficulties the people with OCD are experiencing.

Most of all, family members can be role models for their family members with OCD. They can do the exposures, initially, with the people with OCD to show that the feared consequences do not happen. Of course, you will want them to do the exposures on their own eventually, but modeling can be of great benefit at the start of the therapy. Family members can also work together to be sure that no one in the family is accommodating the OCD. Sometimes people with OCD will try to manipulate someone in their family into helping them with a ritual or giving them reassurance. If family members can work together, then they can assist each other to not give in to the OCD demands, but to present a unified front and work together to challenge it.

Remember that it is the OCD that is being challenged. Of course you love the family member with the disorder, but that does not mean you have to love the OCD. Remind family members with OCD of this, to let them know that in order for you to be helpful, you can no longer help them do rituals but will support them in fighting through their difficulties.

Why does my friend with OCD always say that this will be the last time she does a ritual, when I know that this is not true?

She is probably hoping that you will believe her so that she can relieve some of the anxiety she is feeling about doing the ritual. Rituals are interesting in that respect—they are performed as a way to alleviate anxiety, yet performing them also creates anxiety for some people because they are either embarrassed about doing them or afraid they will not do them correctly and will have to start all over from the beginning.

Your friend is also trying to alleviate some stress that she may perceive you are experiencing; if you were to actually believe that this was her last ritual, then you would overlook it because there would be no more rituals occurring. However, this is almost never the case, and now she has to deal with the fact that she made a promise to you that she will probably not keep, which can create more stress for her and make it even more likely that she will do more rituals in the future. Any time you see a friend performing a ritual, let him or her know that you are aware of it and that you would be happy to help them seek treatment.

What if my partner will not leave the house because he is doing a ritual and we need to be somewhere?

The best response, but hardest to actually do, is to leave without him. You need to recognize that you can support your partner without allowing his OCD to interfere in your life. Of course, do not do this without first warning him that the next time his rituals get in the way of your travel plans, you'll go without him. Let him know that you are not going to passively support his OCD by waiting for him to finish his rituals. Make him aware that his choosing to ritualize instead of leave on time is his choice and that you will not let it interfere with your plans.

When you arrive at your destination alone, you may get questions about where your partner is. You can tell people that he had some things that he needed to finish before he could leave home and then leave it at that.

Chapter 11

TIPS FOR GETTING HELP

- Are there support groups available for OCD sufferers?
- Is it helpful to involve the entire family in treatment?
- Are there resources available on the Internet for people with OCD?
- How do I go about finding a therapist for OCD?
- Are there any current research studies on OCD in which I can participate?
- Are you able to function and live a normal life with OCD?
- Can I donate money to support OCD research and treatment?
- Are health professionals well informed about OCD?
- I want to treat OCD someday—what are my options for becoming a treatment provider?
- What did you mean when you said, "Anxiety is not a fear of a thing; it is a fear of the way you think about a thing"?

Are there support groups available for OCD sufferers?

Yes, there are support groups available for individuals with OCD. One of the best places to find this information is through the Obsessive Compulsive Foundation (OCF), a national association for treatment providers, individuals, and families working and dealing with OCD (www.ocfoundation.org).

According to the OCF, several types of support groups are available:

1. **Professionally assisted groups:** A therapist runs this type of group and leads group therapy. The therapist may use the group as a way to help motivate individuals and hold them accountable for doing exposures, in addition to giving lectures or lessons on how to challenge obsessions and compulsions. There is usually a fee for these groups, which insurance may or may not cover.

2. **Mutual support groups:** The leaders may be individuals with OCD who have recovered or family members of individuals with OCD who want to be able to help others dealing with the disorder. Instead of being therapeutic, these groups help to disseminate information about OCD, such as where to get professional help or what research studies might be ongoing. They may also bring in speakers to teach the group about OCD or something related to it, such as depression or social anxiety. There is often no fee or a small fee for these groups.

3. **Obsessive Compulsive Anonymous:** This is a twelve-step program and is modeled on the first twelve-step program, the well-known one for alcoholism. These groups are purely member-driven, and they typically collect a small fee for the use of the meeting room. As in other twelve-step programs, the

person works through a set of steps and is given a sponsor to assist him or her through each step and any difficult times he or she may have.

4. **Giving Obsessive Compulsive Another Lifestyle (G.O.A.L.) group:** This group involves a mental health professional, but is run by the members. These groups are designed to help individuals continue to do exposures and work on relapse prevention. The professionals assist with any exposure development or ideas, but the bulk of the group time is spent doing exposure therapy with others to mutually assist people in their recovery. There may be a fee involved with these groups depending on how the professional has helped to set up the group.

Is it helpful to involve the entire family in treatment?

It can be very helpful to involve the entire family in therapy. Many people with OCD feel as if they are suffering alone. With the support of the entire family, they can feel encouraged to make the changes needed to improve. But the best part of having the family involved in treatment is the opportunity to get them all on the same page about what to do in response to a ritual or an obsession. When the entire family meets with the therapist, they all can ask questions and get information without hearing it second- or third-hand. And the therapist can work with all of them and teach them about avoidance and reassurance-seeking. The therapist can also design exposures in which the entire family can participate.

Are there resources available on the Internet for people with OCD?

There are numerous resources available for people with OCD on the Internet. A quick search will result in thousands of hits. However, the reliability of many sites can be questionable. For the most up-to-date, research-based information, you may want to look at the following websites:

- The Awareness Foundation for OCD and Related Disorders: www.ocdawareness.com
- The Obsessive Compulsive Foundation: www.ocfoundation.org
- The Anxiety Disorders Association of America: www.adaa.org
- The Association for Behavioral and Cognitive Therapies: www.abct.org
- The Madison Institute of Medicine's OCD Information Center: http://www.miminc.org/aboutocic.asp
- The National Alliance for the Mentally Ill: www.nami.org

How do I go about finding a therapist for OCD?

There are many ways to find a therapist to assist you with your OCD. Several websites focused on behavioral therapy have sections listing specialists. You can look at the following:

- Anxiety Disorders Association of America: www.adaa.org
- Association for Behavioral and Cognitive Therapy: www.abct.org
- Obsessive Compulsive Foundation: www.ocfoundation.org

You can also inquire about a therapist through your employee assistance program, look into local support groups through your local chapter of the National Association of Mental Illness (NAMI), or call a therapist in your area and tell him or her that you want to find a therapist who specializes in the treatment of OCD. This therapist will hopefully have some referrals to give you.

Are there any current research studies on OCD in which I can participate?

Numerous research studies for OCD are ongoing. One easy way to find out what studies are currently recruiting participants would be to go to the Obsessive Compulsive Foundation website (www.ocfoundation.org) and click on the tab that says "Research Participants Sought" under the heading "Information & Resources" on the right side of the page. The OCF keeps a list of research studies focused on OCD, and it also awards grants each year to fund new studies of OCD.

The website of the National Institute of Mental Health (NIMH, at this address: http://www.nimh.nih.gov/studies/studies_ct.cfm?id=9) also lists studies seeking OCD participants. NIMH also gives out research grants to individuals investigating OCD. Only through continued research will we learn more about OCD, find better ways to treat it, and learn how it works in the brain. Offering to participate in these studies can go a long way toward the development of more effective treatments.

Are you able to function and live a normal life with OCD?

You are absolutely able to function with OCD. However, that level of functioning will most likely depend on your follow-through with your therapy and medication regimen. Many patients enter therapy hoping that their therapists will cure them—but if you have OCD, whether or not you get better is really up to you. Your therapist will not cure you. Therapists can give you tools through therapy or prescribe you medications, but following their recommendations is totally up to you.

Following the recommendations of a treatment provider may be one of the most difficult decisions that you will ever make. Some people are opposed to taking medications, so they need to decide to truly commit to taking them if that is the route of treatment that they choose. Or if you are going to do exposure therapy, your therapist is going to ask you to purposely do the very things that you are afraid of, and you have to decide whether you are going to follow through with those exposures. Doing the exposures only 90 percent of the time, will, in the long run, help maintain your OCD because you will have convinced yourself that even though it is not totally correct, part of your OCD (10 percent) is right and therefore still needs to be feared. You need to decide to be 100 percent committed to working on challenging your OCD, or your chances of recovery will decrease. Although it is a challenge, people do it successfully every day, and you have the ability to be successful.

Can I donate money to support OCD research and treatment?

Several groups accept money for OCD support, including the following:

- The Awareness Foundation for OCD and Related Disorders: www.ocdawareness.com
- The Obsessive Compulsive Foundation: www.ocfoundation.org
- The Anxiety Disorders Association of America: www.adaa.org
- The Association for Behavioral and Cognitive Therapies: www.abct.org
- The Madison Institute of Medicine's OCD Information Center: http://www.miminc.org/aboutocic.html

Also, many hospitals that treat OCD have charitable organizations that accept donations on behalf of their OCD treatment programs.

Are health professionals well informed about OCD?

Health professionals could be better informed about OCD, but at least the word is getting out about it. Thanks to many media campaigns and medical advancements, primary care physicians are becoming more aware of OCD and are able to make accurate referrals to psychiatrists and behavioral health providers. Drug companies often visit doctors to let them know of new products for different disorders, such as antidepressant medications (many of which are also effective for OCD). Pharmaceutical companies are also putting ads on television to get information directly to consumers about new medications that are available for treating their difficulties. Additionally, new research is emerging about surgeries that might be helpful for OCD.

Finally, the advances in the treatment of OCD using CBT and ERP are huge. There are people who speak nationally about OCD, entire books published on OCD, and there are specialty treatment clinics in several areas of the country that focus specifically on OCD treatment. As more professionals become informed about OCD, there will be fewer misdiagnoses and quicker treatment available for individuals with OCD.

I want to treat OCD someday—what are my options for becoming a treatment provider?

There are many options for providing treatment to individuals with OCD. You can take a medical route, going to medical school to become either a physician or a psychiatrist. If you do this, you will work mainly in the area of prescribing medications for people with OCD. You can also go to nursing school and work as a psychiatric nurse in a psychiatric hospital treating people with OCD. Some nurses get even further training as nurse practitioners and are able to prescribe medications, often under the supervision of a physician.

Or, you could go to graduate school in the areas of social work, education, counseling, or psychology. You can either get a master's degree and start to work with patients with OCD or go on for your doctorate in any of these fields and work with OCD. After completing your doctorate, you can even do specialized training in OCD during a fellowship.

Other people that treat individuals with OCD may be members of the clergy, chiropractors, expressive therapists (music therapy, art therapy, dance/movement therapy, etc.) or surgeons. While OCD may not have been a major area of their studies, they may work in conjunction with other providers to assist individuals with OCD.

Please recognize that there is considerable cost to going to many of the different schools for careers in the areas mentioned above, although some programs offer free tuition in return for your working for the academic department. It is best to talk to some people who are in the field about how they came to work with OCD so that you can get some different ideas about what route may be the best one for you. Good luck!

What did you mean when you said, "Anxiety is not a fear of a thing; it is a fear of the way you think about a thing"?

The easiest way to explain that saying is to return to our elevator example (see page 126). If we were to perform therapy on a person with elevator phobia, would our goal be to change the elevator, because it is scary, or to change the way the person thinks about the elevator, because they think it is scary?

Our best bet is to go with the second option because there is no way to change an elevator—it will always be an elevator. Instead, what really needs to change is the way you think about the elevator. Your thoughts about the elevator, and nothing else, are preventing you from getting on the elevator. If you thought differently about the elevator, then you would probably ride it, but because you have fear-based thoughts about it, you avoid it. So the goal of therapy is to help you change the way you think about the elevator so that you will stop avoiding it and instead ride it and learn that you can handle it and need not fear it.

Our feelings influence our thoughts, which influence how we behave. So, if we change how we behave, we thereby change our thoughts, and then our feelings will be challenged and will change as well. And that is how to treat OCD.

Appendix A

OBSESSION CHALLENGE WORKSHEET

One way to combat your OCD is to use the following form to help you challenge your obsessive thoughts.

In the first column, list the date, time, and situation where the thought occurred. This will help you establish whether there is a pattern in terms of time of day or situations in which your obsessions occur.

In the second column, list the feelings or emotions that you experience when you have the obsession, and in the third column, list the obsession itself.

In the fourth column, list a response that is a challenge to the obsession. The easiest way to do this would be to think of how someone without OCD, such as your best friend, would think about the obsession.

Further, when you list the emotions, obsessions, and responses, be sure to rate them on a 0–10 scale in terms of how intense the emotions are and the degree to which you believe that the thoughts are true, with 0 being no intensity or no belief in the obsession or response and 10 being the most intense or absolute belief in the obsession or response. For example:

EXAMPLE

OBSESSION CHALLENGE WORKSHEET			
Date, Time, and Situation	Feelings or Emotions (rate intensity on a 0–10 scale)	Obsession (rate belief on a 0–10 scale)	Response (rate belief on a 0–10 scale)
2/25/2007 10:45 a.m. Sitting in church	Anxious (8) Disappointed in myself (7)	If I keep staring at the statue of Jesus, it means that I am attracted to him, and that is a sin. (5)	People stare at religious statues every day as a part of their devotion, and it does not mean that they are attracted to the people the statues represent. (6)
Date, Time, and Situation	Feelings or Emotions (rate intensity on a 0–10 scale)	Obsession (rate belief on a 0–10 scale)	Response (rate belief on a 0–10 scale)

DAILY EXPOSURE HOMEWORK SHEET

This form is designed to help keep you on track with your exposures. There are times when people conveniently "forget" to do their homework, and that can set progress back a great deal—avoidance of exposures can lead to a return of compulsive behaviors. Therefore, this worksheet is designed to help remind you to continue to do your homework and keep exposing yourself to the things that you obsess about.

DAILY EXPOSURE HOMEWORK SHEET

List the obsession that you are going to challenge today. _____

_____

_____

List the compulsive behavior(s) that you perform in response to this obsession. _____

_____

_____

List the alternative behaviors that you plan to perform instead of the compulsive behaviors. _____

_____

_____

How many times did you experience the obsession today? _____

_____

How many times did you perform the alternative behaviors in response to the obsession today? _____

How many times did you perform a compulsion in response to the obsession today? _____

If you did not perform any compulsions, congratulations, and you can work on this or another obsession again tomorrow.

If you did perform compulsions today, why? _____

_____

_____

What will you do to challenge this same obsession tomorrow to increase your chances of not performing any compulsive behaviors in response to this obsession? _____

_____

_____

FEAR HIERARCHY

The fear hierarchy is a way to rank your obsessions and compulsions. For obsessions, consider whether experiencing the thought, impulse, or image brings about a low level of fear, a medium level, or a high level. Or consider whether not performing the compulsion would bring about a low, medium, or high level of fear. An easy way to determine this is to use the following scale:

1	2	3	4	5	6	7	8	9	10
Minimal Fear		Some Fear		Moderate Fear		Significant Fear		Extreme Fear	

Rank low-level fears from 1 to 3.
Rank medium-level fears from 4 to 7.
Rank high-level fears from 8 to 10.

You can list your fears on the hierarchy and it will allow you to expose yourself gradually to your fears, from those with the lowest levels to the highest, by yourself or with a therapist. Do not try to expose yourself to the highest-level fears first—work your way up the hierarchy.

FEAR HIERARCHY FORM

1	2	3	4	5	6	7	8	9	10

Minimal Fear   Some Fear   Moderate Fear   Significant Fear   Extreme Fear

Low-level feared obsessions or incomplete compulsions:

_____

_____

_____

_____

_____

Medium-level feared obsessions or incomplete compulsions:

_____

_____

_____

_____

_____

High-level feared obsessions or incomplete compulsions:

_____

_____

_____

_____

_____

Appendix D THE VERTICAL ARROW

The goal of the vertical arrow is to allow you to get to the core fears that underlie the obsessions that you have. It is a very simple exercise, but can lead to great insight in terms of what your fears are and where they are based.

For example, consider the following scenario:

> *If I do not bleach all of the items that my children touch, they will get sick.*
> If that were true, what would that mean to you?
> *I would be at fault for their getting sick.*
> If that were true, what would that mean to you?
> *I would be a bad mother.*
> If that were true, what would that mean to you?
> *My family would hate me.*
> If that were true, what would that mean to you?
> *I would be unlovable.*

Now look over all the answers that you have written and pick out the themes. These are your core beliefs. What are the core beliefs that you have discovered underlie your obsessions? (Following are the core beliefs held by the person in this scenario about bleaching the childrens' toys. See page 39 and 40 for core belief examples.)

1. *Alienation—Everyone will hate me.*
2. *Worthiness—No one will love me.*
3. *Incompetence—I cannot keep my family safe.*

After you are aware of what your core beliefs are, you can begin to come up with exposures to challenge these beliefs.

VERTICAL ARROW

List an obsessive thought:

_____

_____

_____

_____

If that were true, what would that mean to you?

_____

_____

_____

If that were true, what would that mean to you?

_____

_____

_____

If that were true, what would that mean to you?

_____

_____

_____

If that were true, what would that mean to you?

_____

_____

_____

_____

Now look over all the answers that you have written and pick out the themes. These are your core beliefs. What are the core beliefs that you have discovered underlie your obsessions?

_____

_____

_____

_____

Now that you are aware of what your core beliefs are, you can begin to come up with exposures to challenge these beliefs:

_____

_____

_____

_____

Bibliography

Abramowitz, J. S. (2006). *Understanding and Treating Obsessive-Compulsive Disorder*. Mahwah, NJ.: Lawrence Erlbaum, Associates.

Abramowitz, J. S., & Houts, A. C. (Eds.). (2005). *Concepts and Controversies in Obsessive Compulsive Disorder*. New York. Springer.

American Psychiatric Association. (2000). *Diagnostic and Statistical Manual of Mental Disorders* (4th ed. – text revision). Washington, DC: Author.

American Psychiatric Association (2007). Practice guideline for the treatment of patients with obsessive-compulsive disorder. *American Journal of Psychiatry, 164*(suppl), 1-56.

Antony, M. M., Orsillo, S. M., & Roemer, L. (Eds.). (2001). *Practitioner's Guide to Empirically Based Measures of Anxiety*. New York: Kluwer Academic/Plenum Publishers.

Baer, Lee. (2001). *The Imp of the Mind*. New York. Penguin Group.

Benson, H., Dusek, J. A., Sherwood, J. B., Lam, P., Bethea, C. F., Carpenter, W., Levitsky, S., Hill, P. C., Clem, D. W., Jain, M. K., Drumel, D., Kopecky, S. L., Mueller, P. S., Marek, D., Rollins, S., & Hibberd, P. L. (2006). Study of the Therapeutic Effects of Intercessory Prayer (STEP) in cardiac bypass patients: A multicenter randomized trial of uncertainty and certainty of receiving intercessory prayer. *American Heart Journal, 152*(4), 934-942.

Bernstein, D. A., Roy, E. J., Srull, T. K., & Wickens, C. D. (1991). *Psychology*. Boston: Houghton Mifflin.

Burns, D. D. (1999). *Feeling Good*. New York: Avon Books.

Burns, G. L., Keortge, S. G., Formea, G. M., & Sternberger, L. G. (1996). Revision of the Padua Inventory of Obsessive Compulsive Disorder Symptoms: Distinction between worry, obsessions and compulsions. *Behaviour Research and Therapy, 34*, 163-173.

Clark, C. C. (2006). *Living Well With Anxiety*. New York. HarperCollins.

Croen, L. A., Grether, J. K., Hoogstrate, J., & Selvin, S. (2004). Then changing presence of autism in California. *Journal of Autism and Developmental Disorders, 32*(3), 207-215.

Feldman, R. S., Meyer, J. S., & Quenzer, L. F. (1997). *Principles of Neuropsychopharmacology*. Sunderland, MA.: Sinauer Associates, Inc.

Foa, E. B. & Kozak, M. J. (1995). DSM-IV field trial: Obsessive-compulsive disorder. *American Journal of Psychiatry, 152*, 90-96.

Foa, E. B., Kozak, M. J., Salkovskis, P. M., Coles, M. E., & Amir, N. (1998). The validation of a new obsessive compulsive disorder scale: The Obsessive-Compulsive Inventory. *Psychological Assessment, 10*, 206-214.

Foa, E. B. & Wilson, R. (2001). *Stop Obsessing*. New York: Bantam.

Goodman, W. K., Price, L. H., Rasmussen, S. A., Mazure, C., Delgado, P., Heninger, G. R., & Charney, D. S. (1989). The Yale-Brown Obsessive Compulsive Scale: II. Validity. *Archives of General Psychiatry, 46,* 1012-1016.

Goodman, W. K., Price, L. H., Rasmussen, S. A., Mazure, C., Fleischmann, R. L., Hill, C. L., Heninger, G. R., & Charney, D. S. (1989). The Yale-Brown Obsessive Compulsive Scale: I. Development, use, and reliability. *Archives of General Psychiatry, 46,* 1006-1011.

Grayson, J. (2003). *Freedom From Obsessive-Compulsive Disorder.* New York: Penguin Group.

Helgoe, L. A., Wilhelm, L. R., & Kommar, M. J. (2005). *The Anxiety Answer Book*. Naperville, IL.: Sourcebooks, Inc.

Hodgson, R. J., & Rachman, S. (1977). Obsessive compulsive complaints. *Behaviour Research and Therapy,* 15, 389-395.

Landsman, K. J., Rupertus, K. M. Pedrick, C. (2005). *Loving Someone with OCD.* Oakland, CA.: New Harbinger.

Merriam-Webster's Seventh New Collegiate Dictionary. (1971). Springfield, MA. G. & C. Merriam Co.

Null, G, & Bernikow, L. (2000). *The Food-Mind-Body Connection.* New York, Seven Stories Press.

Obsessive Compulsive Cognitions Working Group. (1997). Cognitive assessment of obsessive-compulsive disorder, *Behaviour Research and Therapy, 35*, 667-681.

Osborn, I. (1999). *Tormenting Thoughts and Secret Rituals*. New York: Random House.

Purdon, C. & Clark, D. A. (2005). *Overcoming Obsessive Thoughts*. Oakland, CA.: New Harbinger.

Webster's NewWorld Stedman's Concise Medical Dictionary. (1987). New York: Prentice Hall.

Websites

- www.worrywisekids.org/anxiety/pandas.html

- www.ocfoundation.org

- www.adaa.org

- www.abct.org

- www.miminc.org/aboutocic.asp

- www.geonius.com/ocd/

- www.who.int/healthinfo/statistics/bod_obsessivecompulsive.pdf

Index

A

acute stress disorder, 95
age and onset of OCD, 22
aggression, 7
agoraphobia, 94, 98
Americans with Disabilities Act
  (ADA), 182–184, 185
ianal retentive,î 127–128
anxiety disorders, 2–3, 92–96,
  220–221
Anxiety Disorders Association
  of America, 16
art therapy, 151
Asperger's disorder, 111
attention deficit-hyperactivity
  disorder (ADHD), 109–110
attention getting, 46
autism, 15, 110–111
Aviator, The, 16

B

bad thoughts, 65–68
bathrooms, 31–32
benzodiazepines (BDZs), 172–173
biofeedback, 136–137
blindness, 197–198
bodily fluids, fear of, 32–33
body dysmorphic disorder
  (BDD), 103–104

C

checking obsessions and compulsions, 6–7
  examples, 41
chemical imbalance, 48–50
cleanliness fixation, 27–28
coexisting conditions, OCD
  and, 114–115
cognitive behavioral therapy
  (CBT), 48, 72, 125–127
cognitive distortions, 128–130
college success and OCD,
  192–193
communicability, 54, 58–59
compulsions, 37–38, 78. See
  also specific types
  defined, 4–5
  mental versus physical, 87–88
contamination obsessions and
  compulsions, 8, 27, 29–30
  examples, 42
  sample hierarchy, 132–133
craziness and abnormality,
  11–12
cutting (self-mutilation), 109

D

dance/movement therapy,
  150–151

D-cycloserine, 174
delusional disorder, 105–106
diagnosis of OCD, 20–22,
    24–25, 124–125
    early signs, 22–23
diet and exercise, 60–61
Dirty Filthy Love, 16
disease versus disorder, 121
dopamine, 167

E

eating disorders, 107–108
endorphins, 165
environmental influences, 58–59
Equal Employment
    Opportunity Commission
    (EEOC), 183–184
exposure and response preven-
    tion (ERP) therapy, 53, 56,
    131–135, 138–139
    side effects, 133–134

F

famous people with OCD,
    16–17
fears and beliefs, 26–27, 51–52
*Feeling Good: The New Mood
    Therapy*, 128
fight or flight response, 59

G

GABA, 167–168, 172
gender and OCD, 11
generalized anxiety disorder

(GAD), 95–96, 97
genes and OCD, 10–11, 57–58,
    191
Giving Obsessive Compulsive
    Another Lifestyle (G.O.A.L.),
    215
As Good as It Gets, 16
growing out of OCD, 10

H

harm obsession examples, 45
health professionals and OCD,
    219
help, getting, 121–125
    family members, 210–211,
    215
    Internet resources, 215–216
    refusal, 208–209
    support groups, 214–215
hepatitis, fear of, 200–202
history of OCD, 14–15
HIV, 80–82
hoarding obsessions and com-
    pulsions, 6, 86–87, 205–206
    examples, 42–43
hurting self and others, fear of,
    180–181, 186–187, 198–200.
    See *also* harm obsession
    examples
hypochondriasis, 106

I

illegal drug use, 176
incidence of OCD, 5, 12–13,
    15–16

inhibitors, 167–168
insurance and OCD, 157–158
intensive outpatient program
    (IOP), 145–146
Internet resources, 215–216

J
job performance and OCD,
    184–186

K
kleptomania, 104

L
licensing, therapy and, 124–125
Lilly Cares Program, 175–176
limbic system, 166
Loving Someone with OCD
    (Landsman), 193

M
major depressive disorder, 112
marriage and OCD, 193–194
Maudsley Obsessive Inventory,
    24
media, 9–10, 16
medical history and develop-
    ment of OCD, 26
medications, 164–165, 174–175
    affording, 175–176
mental disorders, 92
mental retardation, 15
Monk, 16
monoamine oxidase inhibitors
    (MAOIs), 170–171
moral and ethical problems,
    54–55

N
nature versus nurture, 57–60
neuroimaging, 48
neuroleptics, 173–174
neurons, 165–166
neurotransmitters, 49–50,
    165–166, 167–168
norepinephrine, 167

O
obsessions, 33–37. See *also spe-
    cific obsessions*
defined, 3–4
obsessions and compulsions
    examples, 41–45
Obsessive Compulsive
    Anonymous, 214–215
obsessive-compulsive disorder
    (OCD), 9–10, 94–95,
    217–218. See *also* symptoms
    of OCD
    course, 7–8, 195–196
    defined, 2, 5–6
    model, 152–155
    remission, 148
    risk factors, 51
    severity, 7–8
    types, 6–7
Obsessive Compulsive
    Foundation, 13, 122, 214, 217
Obsessive Compulsive

Inventory, 24
obsessive-compulsive personality disorder (OCPD), 116–117
obsessive thoughts, 65–71, 73. See *also specific obsessions*
controlling, 69–70
OCD spectrum disorders, 99

P

Padua Inventory, 24
PANDAS, 55–56
panic attacks, 93, 98–99
parenting and OCD, 189–190, 194–195
partial hospitalization program (PHP), 144–145
perfectionism, 30–31, 80, 82, 83–84
phobias, specific, 94
phobias versus OCD, 95–96
posttraumatic stress disorder (PTSD), 95, 97
psychiatrists, psychologists and, 122–123
punishment from a god, OCD as, 53–54
puppet therapy, 151
pyromania, 104–105

R

reacting to someone with OCD, 209
reassurance-*See*king, 52–53, 64–65

religion, 71–72, 195–196. See *also* spirituality
remission, 148
research on OCD, 217
donating money, 218
reward systems, short- and long-term, 80–82
risk factors for OCD, 51
rituals, 21–22, 29–30, 74, 85–86, 90, 188–189
compared to habits, 23–24
controlling, 204, 211–212
safety-*See*king, 89, 189–190, 204–205

S

scrupulosity obsessions and compulsions, 7, 14, 27, 71–72
examples, 44
selective serotonin reuptake inhibitors (SSRIs), 168–169
serotonin, 166
sexuality, 72–73
situational OCD, 31–32
skin picking, 102–103
social life, OCD and, 181–182
social phobia, 95, 98
spirituality, 156–157. See *also* religion and OCD
strep throat (PANDAS), 55–56
stress levels, 115–116
superstitions, 35–36, 74–75
support groups, 214–215
surgery, 155–156
symmetry obsessions and com-

pulsions, 26, 38, 79–80
  examples, 43–44
symptoms of OCD, 26, 28–29,
  37–40, 82
  substitution, 88
  variation, 178–180
systematic desensitization,
  137–138

T

telehealth, 136
telling others about OCD,
  190–191
therapy, 121, 140–141,
  153–155. See *also specific ther-*
  apies; treatments for OCD
  belief systems, 151–152
  choosing fear, 138
  duration, 147–148
  finding a therapist, 140–141,
  216
  success, 135, 217–218
  technology, 135–136
thought themes, 130–131
tic disorders, 100–101
time devoted to obsessive
  thoughts, 64
Tourette's disorder, 100–101
traditional outpatient therapy,
  146–147
traumatic events, 56–57
treatments for OCD, 8–9, 125,
  142–143, 158–159, 160, See *also*
  specific therapies; under therapy
  hospitalization, 143–144
  insurance, 157–158

nontraditional, 150–151
  physical health, 159–160
  providers, 219–220
  recommending, 207–209
  self-help techniques, 149–150
  testimonials, 160–162
trichotillomania (TTM),
  101–102
tricyclic antidepressants,
  169–170
tryptophan, 61, 166
twins, 57–58

U

unconscious psychological prob-
  lems, 50–51
Understanding and Treating
  Obsessive-Compulsive Disorder
  (Abromowitz), 50

V

virtual reality, 135–136

W

washing and cleaning obsessions
  and compulsions, 6, 13, 16,
  33, 79
  examples, 42
willpower, 5–6
worrying, 112–114

Y

Yale-Brown Obsessive
  Compulsive Scale (Y-BOCS), 24

About the Author

Patrick B. McGrath, PhD, is a licensed clinical psychologist and the director of the OCD and Related Anxiety Disorders Program at Alexian Brothers Behavioral Health Hospital in Hoffman Estates, Illinois. He is also the author of *Don't Try Harder, Try Different*, a workbook for stress management (for information, contact stressmgmt@comcast.net). In addition to providing therapy and writing, Dr. McGrath is  involved in training graduate students in psychology, and he is a member of several national mental health associations. He also performs research and speaks nationally on anxiety disorders. He lives and practices in the Chicago area.